Weathering Life's Storms

How to Push Through When You Want to Give Up

By Pastor Ron McKey

Readable Reach

Edited by Readable Reach, readablereachbooks.com

Weathering Life's Storms: How to Push Through When You Want to Give Up
Pastor Ron McKey. -- 1st ed.

ISBN 978-1-7343301-1-3

CONTENTS

CHAPTER SIX

CHAPTER SEVEN

INTRODUCTION

I t is my prayer that this book you are about to read will give you the tools you need to not only get through life's most difficult seasons, but to come out stronger on the other side.

Everyone experiences ups and downs in life. It is part of being human and living on this earth. But those downs do not have to defeat you. God can use them to make you better, wiser, and more compassionate. He can transform your storm into something that builds you up, if you will let Him.

This book is a collection of sermons preached over several years. As a pastor, I minister to a constant flow of hurting people. I have seen more tragedy and heartbreak than the average person, and my heart breaks along with those of the people I minister to.

However, I have also seen the amazing things God can do *in* people and *through* them as a result of life's storms. He can turn ashes into beauty, and my hope is that this book will help you to come out victorious on the other side of the storms you face.

In the book, I will explain what I mean when I say STORM, how to build a strong life that can withstand a storm, what to do when you are struggling in your marriage or finances, how to battle worry and depression, and finally, how to rebuild after a storm.

We will see what the Bible says about getting through tough times and what Jesus did when He faced the greatest storm of all.

If you are trying to be prepared before a storm, if you are currently in one, or if you have just come out of a storm, this book is for YOU. I want to see you win at life and stay steady through everything that life throws at you. This book is my attempt at giving you resources to do that. May God bless you and give you peace and endurance.

CHAPTER ONE

WHEN STORMS COME

N otice, the title of this chapter is not *if* storms come or *in case* a storm should ever come, or *maybe someday perhaps there is a possibility* you might face a storm. It's *WHEN* Storms Come. Every one of us faces storms throughout life. No one is immune or gets a free pass.

If you are going through a difficult time right now in your marriage, hold on; it's just a storm. You will get through it. Every family goes through storms. It's not that your family is completely dysfunctional. There is a storm brewing, and storms and dysfunction can sometimes look a lot alike.

When I use the word *storm*, I use it as a metaphor to describe difficult days, setbacks, and hard times that we go through. I describe it that way because, as we well know, when a storm blows through, it rearranges our lives. It changes the landscape, and things look different afterward. We even have coined a phrase for it, which is that you have to "figure out your new normal".

So, we understand storms, and everybody goes through them, whether they are emotional, financial, a career change, or a physical storm. Maybe there is pain in your body right now or you are in a relationship storm. Whatever it is, I want you to be encouraged through this book, because I believe that God is going to reveal something to you as you read that will help you learn to weather the storms.

You Are Not Alone

I would like to start by giving you a few verses to let you know you are not alone. In Job chapter five, the Bible says:

Job 5:7

Man is born into trouble.

You cannot get any more black and white than that. When you were born, you were born into an imperfect world, a world where bad things happen to good people. You were born into a fallen world that is filled with trouble. Next is 2 Timothy 3:1, which says:

2 Timothy 3:1

In the last days, perilous, dangerous, difficult times shall come.

I really believe that we are living in the the last days. So, we are experiencing that verse. Then there is Psalms 34:19, which says:

Psalms 34:19

Many are the afflictions of the righteous.

It doesn't say several, a few, or some, but *many* are the afflictions of the righteous. However, God delivers you out of them all.

There is some good news in the midst of your affliction. In John 16:33, Jesus said:

John 16:33

These things have I spoken to you that in me you may have peace. In the world you will have tribulation, but be of good cheer. I have overcome the world.

I could read on and on, verse after verse, making this point that we are *all* going to have troubles in this life, but we know that to be true. Max Lucado, a great author, said this: "Lower your expectations of Earth. This is not Heaven, so don't expect it to be."

In Heaven, there are no problems. In Heaven, there are no storms. In Heaven, you will not fight any battles...but this is not Heaven. And so, until you get there, you are going to go through some difficulty and have to learn how to handle the storms of life.

Let me just say right up front, this is not a book on how bad life is and how much your life stinks. That is not what this is all about. This book is to tell you that you are going to go through storms, but the good news is, you can get through them. God has given us principles from the Bible to help us overcome, and He will be with us to apply those principles. With God, we can get through whatever it is that we have to go through.

S-T-O-R-M

I would like to give you some characteristics of a storm to help you keep a right perspective, and to do that, I made an acronym out of the word STORM.

S-Sudden

For the letter S, here is what I know about storms: They are sudden. They can show up out of nowhere. I mean, one day you are on top of the world, and the next day, the world is on top of you. You know what I mean. It can change that quickly.

When I was in Israel, we were told by our guide that on the Sea of Galilee, storms will form behind the surrounding mountains because the sea sits down in a bowl, so to speak. In Bible times, obviously they did not have the same technology we have to predict them.

So, storms would form behind the mountains and then drop down onto the lake suddenly. People would be out fishing, and everything was smooth sailing. The next thing they knew, they were fighting to stay afloat and struggling just to get back to shore and keep their heads above water.

Well, spiritual storms, life storms, are the same way. Everything is fine one moment. Then, all of a sudden, without warning, without sirens, without any handwriting on the wall, difficult times come. That is why the Bible says that we are to live by faith (Romans 1:17).

Some storms show up so suddenly that you do not have time to build your faith. You do not have time to get prayed up. You had better be prayed up *already* to deal with what you are going to have to deal with.

I have this mental picture in my mind that sometimes, when the storm hits people, they are running around trying to find their helmet of salvation and their shield of faith, or rummaging around trying to find the sword of the Spirit... Wear the armor of God all the time (Ephesians 6), because life comes at you fast. Sometimes it just shows up. Therefore, faith has to be a lifestyle.

T-Temporary

The letter T stands for temporary. I also know that even though storms are sudden, they do not last forever; they are temporary. Inside of your Bible, put a notecard somewhere that says: "This too, shall pass." It is a great thought, but that is not from Scripture. A lot of people think it is, but let me give you the Scripture that the phrase is based on. 2 Corinthians 4:17 is where we get that. It says:

2 Corinthians 4:17

For our present troubles are small and won't last very long. Yet these problems, these troubles, produce for us glory that vastly outweighs the problem and that glory will last forever.

Storms do not last forever, but the *benefits* that you get from the storms do. What you learn from that storm will not only help you in this life, but it will prepare you for the life to come. Storms do not last forever, but the blessing of going through them do.

Robert Schuller used to make this statement: "Tough times don't last, but tough people do¹." Don't lose heart in your storm. There will be an end to it. You are not going to live there forever.

Never go through your storm without hope. You cannot rise any higher than the hope that is on the inside of you, and I really believe that one of Satan's greatest tools that he uses to discourage and to imprison people is to take away their hope of ever seeing the end of the storm, never seeing the light at the end of the tunnel.

Once your hope is gone, you will not survive or thrive. You will not make it. So keep hope alive. You have got to keep believing. Hope is a vision for your future, and the Bible clearly says that where there is no vision, you perish (Proverbs 29:18). If you give up, lie down, and quit, you perish. You have got to have a vision of seeing yourself get out of the storm, walking out of your situation, and having a better life.

O-Opportunities

The letter O stands for Opportunities. Our storms are our opportunities, and for every problem, there is a promise. Whenever you face a storm, God will do a work in you. If you are facing a storm right now, I am confident you are getting ready to experience the presence of God. Someone once said (and rightfully so) that there are three types of people on earth:

1) Those who are in a storm
2) Those who have just come out of a storm
3) Those who are getting ready to walk into a storm

Did you see the cycle there? We are either in a storm, out of a storm, or getting ready to go through a storm. But, our storms can be our opportunities.

I have gone through many storms, and I always know that afterward, I become smarter, stronger, and closer to God than I have ever been. And if I hadn't gone to the storm, I wouldn't have had these lessons.

Now, don't get me wrong; I wouldn't want to repeat them. I did not choose them. But now that I have gone through them, I wouldn't trade anything for what I have learned or the strength that I have gained and being closer to God because of them. I know we do not like going through the storms, but there are blessings that you would never have any other way.

With God, there is no pain without purpose.

There is always a purpose for your pain. I did not say that God brought it. I am just saying that God will get you through it, and there is always a great purpose He will bring out of it. I like the statement, "You'll never be an exceptional person if you fight ordinary battles." Some of you feel like world-class contenders because of the storms you are going through right now.

I love this statement: "If you want to be ranked number one, you can't just beat number nine." There are things in our lives that, because we face them and we get through them, God promotes us.

Think of it this way: God used Goliath to propel David to notoriety. He was just another shepherd boy until he killed the giant. God took that obstacle in his life, that battle, that storm, and He used it to cause him to become the king of Israel.

God used Pharaoh to shape Moses into the incredible leader that even today is still considered the greatest leader Israel has ever had. God used Potiphar's wife in the story of Joseph. She lied about him, and he was thrown into prison. But God used that experience, that storm, and out of it, Joseph became second behind Pharaoh over all of Egypt.

Even Jesus had Judas in his life, and Judas started Jesus toward His destiny of the cross. So, whatever is in your life that is working against you, I promise you, God is going to use it to get you where you need to be, and He will bring good out of your situation.

R-Repeat

The letter R is for Repeat, because some storms repeat themselves. Margaret Thatcher, the former Prime Minister of Britain, said: "You might have to fight a battle more than once to win it." I really think often, that is referring to a stronghold. A stronghold is a an area in our life in which we continually find ourselves fighting against the devil.

There are some battles that, just because you win them, it does not mean Satan isn't going to bring them back around and try to use the same things to defeat you. He will try to find that same weakness, that same chink in your armor, to break you down. And that is why we can never let down our guard. You have got to stay ready to fight that same battle over and over as many times as is needed. The devil never gives up. Therefore, we can never let our guard down.

I like what my friend, Joe McGee said: "Do you know why we're here on Earth? We're here to fight Hell and solve problems. That's it." As a Believer, as a Christian, that is what you do. You are going to fight throughout all of your Christian life. Try to learn to enjoy the battle.

M-Man Made

For the letter M, remember that some of the storms we face in life are man made; we created them ourselves. And if we did not create them, sometimes they came because somebody around us made a decision that affected us. That is why the Bible says, "Pray for those who have authority over you (1 Timothy 2:2)." In other words, "God, the people who are over me and affect my life, don't let them be stupid. God, make them smart. Bless them, and anoint them…"

But, a lot of storms we face are made by us. We sabotage our own lives by our bad decisions and people we let into our lives.

A great example is Jonah. Jonah created his own set of bad circumstances when he disobeyed God. Not only did it affect him, but it affected everyone in the boat with him. Everybody was about to go down on the same ship until God said, "I'm going to fix this."

Jonah's rebellion and desire to do what he wanted to do created a storm in his life. His disobedience put him and others in a bad situation. Your decisions, your lifestyle choices, and who you are do not just affect you; they affect everyone in your life. You may be causing pain to the people who love you most.

Here is some good advice: If you are not happy with your marriage, look in the mirror. Talk to *that* person. Your spouse is a reflection of you. Husbands, Wives, if you do not like the way you look, dress differently; act differently. Do something to change it.

Dr. Dave Martin, a motivational speaker and great Christian brother in the Lord, made this statement: "There are two types of people in life. There are drivers, and there are passengers. The drivers are the ones who take the wheel, are looking forward, and are continually making adjustments. They are thinking about where they are going, and they have charted a course. Passengers are the ones who just sit there and let other people drive their life." You want to be in the driver's seat; trust me. You want to take control. You want to chart the course of your life.

Anchors from God

Look in your Bible at Acts chapter 27. This is one of the great storms of the Bible. This is about the Apostle Paul, and he gets caught up in a storm. In fact, the Bible says that this storm was so bad, they had not seen the sun during the day or the stars during the night for 14 days. That is a storm! I mean, wherever they looked, all they could see was darkness and clouds. During the day, they could not see the sun, and at night, they could not see the stars. The Bible says:

Acts 27:27-29

When the fourteenth night had come, as we were being driven across the Adriatic Sea, about midnight the sailors suspected that they were nearing land. So they took a sounding and found twenty fathoms. A little farther on they took a sounding again and found fifteen fathoms. And fearing that we might run on the rocks, they let down four anchors from the stern and prayed for day to come.

I want to look at some anchors that God has given us to survive our storms. Here is the thing about an anchor: The function of it is that if you don't want to drift, if you don't want to crash on shore, if you don't want to slip away, you drop an anchor, and it holds you in that position. God has put some anchors in our lives to hold us and to help us weather the storms.

Family

The first anchor that God has given us is family. You cannot get through storms without family. God has given us our families to help us get through the difficulties we are going to face. It could be flesh and blood family or a church family; God puts people in our lives that we can look to as anchors.

One of the greatest anchors that God has given anyone is the marriage covenant. I like that word *covenant,* because it is not just a marriage contract or a marriage agreement; it is a covenant, meaning that it cannot be broken. It is something that has been thought through and that you have given your whole self to. The Bible says that a three-stranded cord is not easily broken (Ecclesiastes 4:12). So, a marriage is not just two people coming together, it is two people coming together *in the sight of God*, and God is the third cord.

I could use an example of a three-legged stool. If you take away one of the legs and you just have 2 legs, it is not going to be very stable or strong. If you just have two people coming together trying to figure things out by themselves, it is going to be unstable until you put that third leg underneath it. That third leg is God. Now you can trust it. Now there is some stability in what you are doing.   A n d that is what God is saying. He is involved in that marriage, and it becomes an anchor. Matthew 19, verse six says this:

Matthew 19:6

So that they are no longer two, but one flesh. What therefore God has joined together, Let no man put asunder.

The Bible promises supernatural power to two people when they come together. There is no greater anchor for any storm than a marriage covenant, two people being yoked together. When you are holding hands with your spouse, it's more than just a romantic gesture. I want you to think about that next time you are holding hands with your spouse. Your spouse is an anchor. If you get to thinking wrong and wandering off, like toward another man or woman or toward your own vision and doing your own thing, you have an anchor that keeps you and pulls you back in.

My wife, Carol, is my anchor. She is that thing that God has given to me to keep me on course. That is part of the purpose of marriage, and if for any reason we start to wander off or drift emotionally or spiritually, we are there to hold on to each other and be an anchor in every storm.

The next time you are walking with your wife or your husband, holding hands, just realize what an incredible gift God has given you to hold you on course, to finish your course, and run your race. I love 1 John 5:4. Here is the proof:

1 John 5:4

For whatsoever is born of God overcomes the world. This is the victory that overcomes the world, even our faith.

Marriage is a God thing. I mean, God thought it up. God created it. It is something that God has given us. That Scripture says not *whosoever* is born of God but *whatsoever*. A marriage is a God thing. He thought it up, birthed it, created it. And the last half of that verse says, "This is the victory that overcomes the world, even our faith."

Your marriage is born of God. It will stand the storm, and it is an anchor for whatever you are going through. Deuteronomy 6:6 says:

Deuteronomy 6:6

And these words which I command you this day shall be in your heart. You should teach them to your children, and you shall talk of them when you're in your house, when you go for a walk, when you go to bed, when you wake up, write them on the doorpost of your home.

Not only does it apply to marriage; God has given these incredible families to anchor us, and so many people have cut the line to that anchor. God has put you in a family and raised you in that family for a purpose. Those are people in your life who you do not ever outgrow. They are there to be anchors in your life to help you get through.

Whatever reason you cut that line (maybe it is dysfunction in your family or just not valuing your family), you have got to get connected to family in some way. God has put them there to hold you in place and to get you through that storm. And He is saying that you pass this on. Your home is a refuge. It is a place where you speak the Word morning, noon, and night. We never stop doing that. We never stop being an anchor. We never stop being steadfast for our families.

No matter how big our kids get or how old they get, we are there to say, "I am here. I am going to help you get through this storm." We fight Hell, and we solve problems all of our life. We are called to provide spiritual leadership.

First, you give your kids roots, and then you give them wings. Wings without roots will lead to failure. Storm-proof your home. Guard your home. Pray for your family. Stay connected to your family.

Faith

Anchor number two is the anchor of faith. Now, I know all of us have heard sermons on faith. I grew up cutting my teeth on the Word of Faith message, but let's try to see it with some fresh eyes. We have all heard sermons of having faith in God, the value of faith, and the importance of faith. But I am afraid that sometimes it's just become something we have heard so many times, that we ignore it. Maybe we have cut the anchor to faith. Maybe we have drifted from it, and we're looking for some sort of new revelation.

But here is my heart: Let's get back to having faith in a God who can do anything but fail. Let's get back to a place where, when we face a storm in life, the first thing that rises up in our heart and comes out of our mouth is the word of faith that calls those things which be not as though they were. Let's get back to the simple, yet powerful, message of faith. Here are a couple of verses for you:

Hebrews 11:6

But without faith, it is impossible to please him, for he that comes to God must believe that he is and that he is a rewarder of those who diligently seek him.

Mark 9:29

According to your faith, it will be done unto you.

There is verse after verse of all the incredible things God has given to us through faith. Lester Summrall was a great man of faith, and he made this statement: "Faith is an eye that sees the invisible. Faith sees through the storm. Faith sees what others do not see."

D. L. Moody made this statement: "If God says anything, faith says 'I believe it.'" And maybe one of my favorite quotes on faith is from Marilyn Hickey, which says: "Faith clamps down the teeth of God's Word on the seat of the enemy's pants and hangs on until Satan quits."

Sometimes you have just got to out-faith the devil. Sometimes, you've just got to be stronger. Look at Mark 4:37. This is another great storm, and I just want to draw a couple of principles out of it.

Mark 4:37-40

*And a great windstorm arose, and the waves were break-
ing into the boat, so that the boat was already filling. But
he was in the stern, asleep on the cushion. And they woke
him and said to him, "Teacher, do you not care that we are
perishing?" And he awoke and rebuked the wind and said
to the sea, "Peace! Be still!" And the wind ceased, and
there was a great calm. He said to them, "Why are you so
afraid? Have you still no faith?"*

What I want you to focus on for just a moment is the fact that
Jesus spoke *to the storm*. In that moment, Jesus spoke not to God, but
to the storm in front of Him. Mark 11:23-25 says that whoever says to
that mountain, "Be thou removed" and believes and does not doubt in
his heart, that mountain is going to move.

Jesus spoke to stuff! You might say, "Pastor, I don't believe in
speaking to stuff." All right, fine. Do me a favor. Take your Bible, tear
that page out, and throw it away. Then there is not a problem. What
you're saying is, "I don't believe what God says."

I love telling a story about a young lady who came to church
one day. She was walking in, and the pastor looked under her arm. All
she had was just the leather flaps of her Bible. The pastor said,
"Ma'am, I'm sorry, but I think your Bible fell out somewhere. All you
have is to cover." She replied, "No, I've been coming to your church
for about four or five years now, and every time you say, 'Well, that's
not for us today,' I just tear that page out of my Bible. This is all I
have left."

Either we believe it, or we don't. We do not get to choose
cafeteria Christianity. If the Bible says it, let's believe it. On the sub-

ject of faith, Jesus spoke to the storm. Let me break this down and show you why this is so important: Words contain our faith.

Words release our faith. What you believe, you speak, because whatever is coming out of your mouth is the very content of your heart. And when people say, "Look man, you know my heart," I just have to say, "No, I don't. I just know your words. All I know is what's coming out of your mouth. I don't know your heart. I only know what you are telling me. Out of the abundance of the heart, the mouth speaks."

Whatever is in your heart is what you're going to speak in faith, either good or bad. Those are your beliefs. That is what you're holding on to. If you were to take a lady's purse, open it up, and turn it upside down, first you would be shocked. But once you got over the shock (*How can they fit that much stuff in their purses?!*) you'd real-ize that those are some of the things that she thinks are important.

There would be some photographs in there. There definitely would be some makeup and all of her cards... all of these things that she feels like she's got to carry with her. What's in your heart is what comes out of your mouth. The things that you say, the words that you speak, that is who you are. That is where your faith level is. Romans 10:8-10 says:

Romans 10:8-10

But what does it say? The word is near you. It's in your mouth. It's in your heart. That is the word of faith, which we preach, that if you confess with your mouth the Lord Jesus Christ and believe in your heart that God has raised him from the dead, you will be saved. For with the heart

one believes unto righteousness, and with the mouth, con-
fession is made unto salvation.

Now here is the point that I want to bring from that: The greatest miracle that ever will happen and ever has happened is the miracle of the new birth. There is no greater miracle than somebody giving their heart to Christ, and that miracle happens when somebody believes in their heart and then makes a public confession of that belief. That is how you get born again. That is the greatest miracle that you'll ever experience.

Everything else you ever get from God, you get the same way. What you believe in your heart, when you are pressed or pressured, comes as an expression out of your mouth. That takes confession to a whole new level.

When you are pressed and pressured, you really find out who you are and what is in your heart. I encourage you to have faith in God. Have faith in your heart.

The Supernatural

Anchor number three is the anchor of the supernatural. There is a supernatural side of life, and God is just waiting for us to tap into it. It is available for the Believer. I have often said that we live in two worlds simultaneously. We live in a world that is visible, that we can see and touch. But we also live in a world that is invisible, that is supernatural.

It is just as real as the world we are living in right now. We live in a world that is natural and supernatural, that is visible and invisible. There is a God, and there is a devil. There are angels, and there are demons. There are two worlds. One is working for you, and the other is working against you.

If you do not get that, if you do not understand that, then you are defeated before you even start. Let me share with you what the supernatural looks like. Let me give you just a glimpse into that world. Here is what supernatural is: the power of prayer, something God has given us.

I call it the umbilical cord to Heaven. It is our connection, our conduit from Heaven to Earth, and God meets our needs through prayer. We have the Holy Spirit. Frances Chan, an author and a pastor, calls the Holy Spirit the forgotten person of God because sometimes we don't really understand the Holy Spirit. And so we just push Him to the side.

We understand God the Father. We understand Jesus, our Savior. But the Holy Spirit, we do not really understand. Let me encourage you; you need to develop a relationship with the Holy Spirit. You need to know who He is. He is your comforter. He is your keeper. He is your strength. He is your instructor. He is your mentor. He is your help in trouble. He is your guide.

You cannot live a life separate from the Holy Spirit. The church age is all about Him. Build a relationship with Him. The angels of God, what many call God's secret messengers and secret agents, are available. If you do not believe in angels, I want you to know, you are missing out. Every one of us has an angel watching over us. They protect, guide, and comfort us.

I have heard so many stories of missionaries and other people who were in difficult places and literally saw the angels of God to deliver them from the situation and the circumstances that they were in.

There is this thing called the anointing of God, and we say it this way, somewhat jokingly, but not really: The anointing of God is when God puts his super on your natural, when there are things that you cannot do on your own, and God divinely gives you assistance, whether it is witnessing to someone or power in prayer. God might be anointing your prayer life, and you are praying like you never thought you could pray before.

Whatever it is, there are times when God will add His power into your life, and your strength is not enough. God will add to it through this thing called the anointing of God.

There are also the gifts of the Holy Spirit. There are miracles, signs and wonders. All of that is out there waiting for the church, for the Believer, to tap into.

God is a miracle-working God, and just for the record, let me say that I believe in miracles. I believe in things that cannot be explained any other way than to simply say it was a God thing. From Genesis to Revelation, your Bible is a miracle book. It begins with the miracle of creation, that God supernaturally by the power of His words, created the universe and everything around us.

There are miracles of deliverance, that people were in impossible situations, that the odds were stacked against them. And time after time, God delivered them out of a seemingly impossible situations.

He still does the same thing. So if you are in an impossible situation and you do not see any way out, I challenge you and encourage you to believe in the supernatural, because God can make a way out when there seems to be no way out.

There are miracles of healing. There are miracles of provision. There are miracles of guidance, and God is the same yesterday, today and forever. He has not changed. All of these things are available if we will slow down and live a life looking into and tapping into the supernatural. I want us to live a miracle lifestyle, and let me emphasize the word *lifestyle*. A miracle lifestyle is where we expect a miracle.

A number of years ago when Oral Roberts built ORU, so many miracles had to happen that the theme of their school became "expect a miracle". What a great way to live life, having a spirit of expectancy!

Let me explain to you what that is like. Imagine you are expecting a package from FedEx or UPS. You really expected it to show up yesterday. You go three or four times to the front porch to see if it is there, and you even pray for the UPS driver. "God, don't let him have a bad day. God, I pray for him."

You have the spirit of expectancy that it is going to show up, and that is how you live. A miracle life is that you have this expectancy, that God is about to move and do something. You have this thing in your heart, and you believe God is up to something. Expect a miracle.

The word *expect*, according to Webster's dictionary, means "confident an event will happen; looking forward to something taking place". Then I looked up the word *miracle* in the dictionary, and it says, "a supernatural event due to divine intervention".

Now, that is okay if all you have is a dictionary. But if you have a Bible, I believe it can do better. Let me give you a Bible definition. A miracle is a divine invasion of God's unlimited power into this material world that overrides natural laws or circumstances.

In other words, a miracle is a manifestation of God's power into your life. The God of the natural and the God of the supernatural are the same God. Whatever you see, whatever you experience in this world that is good, every good and perfect gift comes down from the Father above. Whatever you have experienced in this life that is good is a God thing. That is the natural side of God, the blessings that he pours out on us.

The God of the natural and the God of the supernatural are the same. And when you develop your faith and come to a place that you believe in the supernatural the way you believe in the natural, you will have a miracle in your life.

We have a natural law called the law of gravity, and every one of us understands that if you go up on the roof of a church and jump off, you will fall to the ground. That is an expectation that we have. We do not expect somebody to jump off the roof of the church and float away. We know what is going to happen. No one is going to be surprised or shocked.

When you begin to have that type of expectation, saying God can and will do something supernatural in your life, and you have it with such a divine confidence, you will begin to live a miracle lifestyle. Let me show you how to position yourself for a miracle.

Understand Your Situation

Number one: Understand your situation. That just simply means to ask yourself the questions, *How did I get here? How did I end up in this situation? What brought me to this place that I need a miracle in my life? Is there something that I did?* Psalm 139 says:

Psalm 139:23-24

Search me, O God, and know my heart! Try me and know my thoughts! And see if there be any grievous way in me, and lead me in the way everlasting!

Do not keep doing the wrong thing that is pushing you further and further away from God. Look at yourself. Check yourself before you wreck yourself, and find out God is there. Is there something you need to do to make that adjustment in your life to position yourself for a miracle?

Forgive

Number two: You are going to need to forgive. Why is that so important? Mark 11:25 says:

Mark 11:25

And whenever you stand praying, forgive, if you have any-thing against anyone, so that your Father also who is in heaven may forgive you your trespasses.

That is pretty black and white. If I refuse to forgive, and if I choose to hold on to and harbor bitterness and anger in my life, it sep-arates me, and I will never live a miracle lifestyle. It separates me from having an effective prayer life. So, I have got to come to the place that says, "You know what, God? I'm going to forgive and let go of those things."

A Spirit of Expectation

Number three: Have a spirit of expectation. That means any day now, I have got high expectations that God is going to come through and see me through the storm.

There is a supernatural side of God. There is this anchor of the supernatural that we experience. There are the angels of God. There is prayer, this incredible thing that God has given us. When we pray, God answers. Prayer is not just some sort of verbal exercise that God has given us to relieve the tension of our life. Prayer is a tool, and God says, "If you pray, I will answer."

If you are going through something and you haven't prayed yet, the greatest thing you can do is stop, hit the pause button in your life, and just say, "God, before I do anything else, I'm going to pray about my circumstance and about my situation." The supernatural side of God is waiting for us. God is going to give you strength in your storm.

The Church

The fourth anchor is the anchor of the church. I love the local church. It would be hard to imagine how many lives have been changed and saved because of the local church. It would be hard to put a number on how many people have received strength, help and encouragement because of a local church, how many marriages have been restored and put back together, or how many tragedies have been diverted simply because there is a place called the church where people can come and get connected to God.

The greatest life support you will ever have in life is a local church. The church is a harbor in a time of storm. Get connected to a church that will hold you in place while you are going through storms. I firmly believe in the local church. The church is a place where you can go and not be criticized for making a mistake.

We talked about the fact that some storms are man made, when we have made some poor choices. Or maybe people in our lives that we have associated with have made choices that have affected our lives. The church is a place where you can come with your mistakes without fearing that someone is going to criticize you because of what is going on in your life.

In the church, we are all equal. There is no hierarchy. There is no pecking order. I love this illustration of King David in the Old Testament. You do not have to be a student of Hebrew or the Old Testament to understand this. The Ark of the Covenant was a place where God's presence was manifested. God did not live in that little box. I think it's funny that even today we still try to put God in a box.

The Ark of the Covenant was a place where God would manifest His power for Israel, and it had been gone, taken away. Finally, it was returning back home to the kingdom. David was so excited because there was a blessing that came with the presence of God.

King David saw the Ark coming, and he walked with it as it came through the processional into the city. He took off his crown and his kingly robes, and he began to dance in front of the Ark. He was as common as anyone else in the kingdom in that moment. Nothing stood out about him.

No matter who you are or what you are, when we get into the presence of God, it is not about us anymore. It is all about Him and what He is doing. That is why I love the church. No matter where you are, we all stand on equal ground, because church is not about us. It is about Christ.

Now, here is a message from that scene. David lay down his title, his occupation, and his identity so that he could get lost in God's identity. See, the church should be a place where you can bring your hurt even in a time of storm, even in a time of crisis. You can show up with your addiction, with your brokenness, with the messiness of your life, and give it to God for healing.

We have got to create a culture where people can bring in with them all of their hurts and hang ups and say, "I'm here to get fixed because I'm broken." We are here not to judge, but to help.

Who hasn't been in a place of needing help? Church is that healing place where people can be restored and be ministered to. Let God turn your mess into your message. If we took time for people to just get up and tell their story, you would be blown away at what God has done.

One of the most quoted Scriptures that we have in church is John 3:16. "For God so loved the world..." Sometimes it is difficult for us to get our minds around this world thing, because it's a big, wide world. It just simply means that God loves others.

God wants to use you to impact other people's lives. God loves others. -the people you work with, go to school with, and that you encounter day to day. God loves those people who are in front of you, near you, and next to you. And God wants to use you to show His love to others. The church isn't a building; it is individuals, and God will use the church to take Jesus to others and to show love to others through us.

So, here is a great question to ask yourself: Did I contribute to another person getting blessed today? In other words, did I serve God today in such a way that others could be blessed?

If you are going through a storm, the greatest thing you need, the most important thing you need, is the presence of God. God has called us to come boldly before the throne of grace. God has called us to come boldly into the Holy of Holies.

When we show up in church, we need to come with a confidence that God is going to show up and do something in our lives. Lay aside anything, any distraction that prevents you from worshipping God and come boldly to the throne of God.

If you have ever traveled, you will know this picture of when you get off the airplane and everybody is waiting by the baggage terminal for their bags to show up. And as soon as their bags show up, they race to the front of the line, elbow their way through, grab their bag, and get out of there.

Spiritually, we often come to church with all of this baggage, and we are like the spiritual baggage collector that is just going round and round. We've got to get our baggage before anybody else does.

I encourage you that when you go to church, leave your baggage outside. You are not going to need it for an hour, and at the end of the service, if you decide that you want it, you can pick it up on the way out. If you've got spiritual baggage (hurts, hang ups, doubts...) just leave it outside, and for an hour, let God change you. Draw near to God, and enter into His presence.

Review

To review, remember that you are not alone in the storms that you face in life. Everyone goes through them. They are temporary, and God can use them for good. To get you through along the way, He has given four anchors that keep us grounded and give us strength: family, faith, the supernatural, and the church. Invest in each of these, and they might one day be lifesavers.

In the next chapter, we will look at how to build your life on a solid foundation, so you can stand strong when rain, floods, and winds come.

Take Action

1. Reflect on how God has helped you through a particular storm in the past.

   _____

   _____

   _____

2. Develop a daily practice of reading the Bible and praying.

CHAPTER TWO

WISE OR OTHERWISE?

D o you want to have a life that is built on a solid foundation? Let's look at Matthew chapter seven and a parable Jesus taught about two builders.

Matthew 7:24-27

Everyone then who hears these words of mine and does them will be like a wise man who built his house on the rock. And the rain fell, and the floods came, and the winds blew and beat on that house, but it did not fall, because it had been founded on the rock. And everyone who hears these words of mine and does not do them will be like a foolish man who built his house on the sand. And the rain fell, and the floods came, and the winds blew and beat against that house, and it fell, and great was the fall of it."

In this parable, we have two builders, one wise and one foolish. We also have two houses. One was built on a good foundation; the other was built on a bad foundation. And then there are two outcomes. One was successful, and the other was a tragedy.

Every one of us, in some way or another, is building a house (or we could say building a life). And everything about what we are doing has to do with the foundation we are building on. Now, I am not a builder, but if I ever build a house, I want a builder who doesn't take shortcuts. I want a builder who doesn't cut corners and doesn't use cheap material. I would plan on living in that place with my family for a long time, and I would want it to be something dependable.

Well, the same is true if you are building a *spiritual* house, or life. You cannot cut corners in becoming a spiritually mature person. There are no shortcuts in this walk and life that we are building with God.

Now, this parable that Jesus taught is not a parable about how to *avoid* a storm, because we all know that we can't. It is a parable to show us how to survive when the storm comes, and it has everything to do with the foundation that we build on. In fact, the heart of this parable is:

Unless God builds the house, you are building in vain.

Unless God is involved in the building process, whatever life you are building, if you are not building it around God, you are really not building a very strong life. It may look good from the outside, but as you get closer, upon inspection, you begin to see all of the flaws.

If you are building without God, literally, all you are doing is building a house of cards. You are just building something that is not going to survive. If you are going to build your life without God and have not involved Him in the process, when tragedy comes, do not blame Him.

There are two men in the story. Jesus called one of them a wise man, and He called the other a moron. It is very interesting, because the Greek word for foolish is the word *moros,* where we get our word *moron*. Now, these two men are a lot alike, so this is not a parable about a bad man and a good man; it is a parable about two men who have a lot of things in common. They both want to build a house. They both have the same teacher. Jesus has given them the same life principles, and they both go through the same storm. The difference is that one built on a foundation of rock, and the other built on a foundation of sand.

They had the same vision, the same message, and the same storm. But, something happened. What was the difference? One was a hearer of the Word, and the other was a hearer AND a doer of the Word. I wish I could tell you that because you come to church and are faithful to the church, when a storm comes, you'll be okay. But, I can't tell you that. It is not your church attendance that gets you through the storm. It is not that you are a good person. The question is, are you *doing* what you are hearing?

It is not just being in church and being faithful. Those are good things, but are you putting into practice what it is that you are hearing? Those are the things that will storm-proof your life.

So, both men faced the same storm. One was a hearer and a doer. One used what I call "WWJD Construction"; he lived his life saying, "What would Jesus do in this situation?" The other built from, "I Can Do it Myself Construction". In other words, "I've got my own ideas, and I'm going to do what I want to do."

You don't survive storms just because you go to church. You survive storms because you are a hearer and a doer of the Word. In fact, if you go back to verse 24, it says in our text:

Matthew 7:24

Therefore, whoever hears the sayings of mine...

Something that I learned back in Bible school is that when you read the Word of God and you find a *therefore*, go back and find out what it is *there for.* It is very significant here, because Jesus is teaching the Sermon on the Mount in Matthew chapters 5-7. Jesus is doing all of this incredible preaching about salt and light, forgiveness, prayer, fasting... and He is giving life principles that we need to live by.

He is showing, "This is how you want to live your life." There are so many great sermons there. The Beatitudes are in that teaching, and at the very end of all of that teaching, He throws in this parable. Here is what He is saying: "If you listen to what I'm saying, and you build on everything else that I just taught you in chapters 5-7, that will be a firm foundation. But if you just hear these things like you would in a church service and you do not do anything with them, you have missed the foundation."

Jesus is the foundation of everything we are building. He is saying, "If you follow my words and my advice, you can build a strong life."

Here is the point: You build the life that you want. You don't just *have* the life you want; you don't just *get* the life you want. You *build* it.

B-U-I-L-D

I want to take the word BUILD and break it down. People ask me, "Pastor, why do you always do that?" I do it because it always helps some people to get it if I put it in some sort of formation.

B- Buy Into

The B stands for *Buy Into*. You are never going to build the life you want until you buy into the fact of following these principles. It is not just a belief system that helps you, but it is *buying into* that belief system.

I was in prayer one day, and God said, "One of the greatest things that you can do for yourself is to believe your beliefs." Do not just say, "Yeah, I believe that," but *believe* your beliefs. Have a heart-felt conviction to say, "Not only do I acknowledge that, but I believe that with my whole heart." One of the best things you can do to grow up spiritually, to grow spiritually mature, is to buy into your beliefs.

Jesus said, "You do not build a house or barn until you first count the cost. That is called buying into. *Do I really want to make this investment? Am I really serious about doing this?* If you are going to build the life you want, there is going to be an investment. There is going to be a cost. In fact, Luke chapter six records a parable. It says that this man dug down deep to build a foundation.

What He is saying is, if you are going to build the life you want, you have got to dig down. It is going to cost you finances, and the deeper you go, the more it will cost you. It is going to cost you strength. It is going to cost you time. It is going to take some discipline. But what you invest in withstands the storm. No shortcuts. Be in it to win it. Focus on building a life.

U- Understand

The letter U stands for *Understand*. Not only do you need to buy into the vision, but you need to understand. Jesus consistently said, "Whoever has ears to hear, whoever hears the sayings of mine and does them, whoever has ears to understand and hears what the Spirit is saying, to them I will give victory (Matthew 11 and 13)." The Greek word for understand means "to renew the mind". It has got to become the way that you think. It has got to become your central focus.

Your mind, or your thoughts, will either take you *toward* your goals in life and the life that you want to build, or your way of thinking is going to take you *away* from the life that you want to experience. We are a byproduct of our thoughts. That's why Proverbs says in chapter 23:

Proverbs 23:7

As a man thinks, so is he.

You are a total product of what you thought about yesterday or last year, and you are today where you are because of your thinking. But the incredible thing is, Jesus said that if you change your thinking, you can change your life.

You have got to do more than just hear the Word. You have got to understand it and meditate on it. Your thoughts determine your destiny, and it is time to take your thinking to the next level, because your old way of thinking is not going to get you where you need to go. Every one of us needs to raise the bar, start thinking God-thoughts, and renew our minds. Ask yourself, "What does the Bible say? What are its foundational truths?"

I- Ignore

The letter I is for *Ignore*. When I put this word down, I thought of Nehemiah, because he really fits this whole subject of storms. Here was a guy who was rebuilding after destruction. The storm of Babylon came; Jerusalem had collapsed, and he knew the value of a wall. A city without a wall meant that it could not keep the enemies out.

Any enemy could come in and capture the city, and Nehemiah said, "We've got to rebuild the wall." When Nehemiah began to re-build, he had to ignore all of the distractions that came along while he was rebuilding. There was a guy in the story by the name of Sanballat. Now, Sanballat represents distraction; he represents the enemy.

The whole time Nehemiah was trying to build, this other guy from another army and another nation kept coming over and saying, "Don't build the wall. This is foolish. Think about what you're doing. It is a bad investment. It is a bad time to do it. Come down off the wall, and talk to me." But every time Sanballat showed up, Nehemiah would not come down off the wall.

The Bible is pretty funny here because it says that Sanballat would go and tell Nehemiah, "Let's go to the Valley of Ono so that we can reason and talk this thing through."

Now, every time the enemy comes and says, "Stop doing what you're doing," you should say, "Oh no. I'm going to stay on the wall and keep building."

Avoid and ignore all of the distractions. You have to ignore every negative person. You may have to ignore every negative situation and everyone else's opinion of what you're doing, and just stay focused on what God has said and what you feel like you need to do to build the life that God wants you to have. You may have to put on spiritual blinders.

They put blinders on horses to keep them focused ahead rather than seeing every distraction to the left and to the right. It limits their vision, and sometimes we need spiritual blinders, because the world is constantly pulling us in different directions. We have this huge attraction to distraction. We are just going along, and "Bird! Squirrel!"

We are focusing on God, running our race, and all of a sudden, we get side-tracked. But we need to put on the spiritual blinders so we can say, "God, I will run *my* race."

L- Labor

L is for Labor, because it takes effort to build the life that you want. The Bible says that whatever you put your hand to will prosper (Deuteronomy 28:8), but the key here is that you have to *do* something.

I had a Bible teacher who used to say, "God won't bless lazy Christians." Whatever you put your hand to, God said, "I will bless it," and part of that means I have got to make myself available to God. Let's read Psalms 1. It is a great psalm about staying on track, avoiding distraction, and building the life that you want. Here is what the Amplified Bible says:

Psalms 1:1-4

Blessed [fortunate, prosperous, and favored by God] is the man who does not walk in the counsel of the wicked [following their advice and example],

Nor stand in the path of sinners,

Nor sit [down to rest] in the seat of scoffers [ridiculers].

But his delight is in the law of the Lord,

And on His law [His precepts and teachings] he [habitually] meditates day and night.

And he will be like a tree firmly planted [and fed] by streams of water, Which yields its fruit in its season;

Its leaf does not wither;

And in whatever he does, he prospers [and comes to maturity].

The wicked [those who live in disobedience to God's law] are not so, But they are like the chaff [worthless and without substance] which the wind blows away.

The Message Bible says:

How well God must like you! You don't hang out at Sin Saloon. You don't slink along Dead End Road. You don't go to Smart Mouth College. Instead you thrill to God's

Word. You chew on Scripture day and night. You are a tree replanted in Eden, bearing fresh fruit every month never dropping a leaf, always in blossom. You're not like the wicked who are mere windblown dust without a defense in court, unfit company for innocent people. God charts the road you take. The road they take is Skid Row.

You have to stay focused on where God is taking you and work with Him to get you there.

D-Daily

Finally, the letter D is for Daily, because it is not what you do just once that changes your life; it is what we do daily. It is not that one-time event that is life changing, but it is what we do day in and day out. Our lifestyle might seem boring or mundane, but every day that we get up, serve God and just do the right thing, it steadily builds a great life.

Rain, Floods, and Wind

Now, back to Jesus' parable. The two men are building a foundation, and it says that when the foundation and houses are built, the storm comes. Now, there are three elements in the storm: rain, floods, and wind. And each one means something different.

Rain

Rain represents problems. Into every life, a little rain must fall. Rain represents those little things in life that we all go through. In fact, I read a book called *Successful Problem Solving,* and in that book, it says that the average person faces 23 problems per day.[2] What if you are above average? I have had those days where 23 would be nice! And I often don't just have my problems; I get *a lot* of people's problems.

We think, "Man! I just need a break!" But 23 problems a day is what the average person faces. We need to learn to become successful problem solvers. Remember, my friend Joe McGee said we are here on this Earth to fight Hell and fix problems. Earth is not Heaven. This is training for eternity, and that is what we do day in and day out.

Remember Nehemiah building the wall. When you read that story, you find out that he had a trowel in one hand and a sword in the other. What is he doing? He is fixing problems and fighting Hell. He is dealing with life and fighting off the enemy the whole time.

So, rains come for everyone, and you need to learn how to solve problems. Here is a great reference. You might want to make this your next tattoo. Psalms 50:15 says:

Psalms 50:15

Call on me in the day of trouble, and I will deliver you.

And here is one for the other arm:

Psalm 46:1

God is our refuge and strength, an ever present help in time of trouble.

Do you realize that there is not a problem that exists that God does not either have a principle or a promise for? It may simply be, "Put God first. It might be, "Seek first the Kingdom of God. Then all of these things will be added unto you (Matthew 6:33)."

And seriously, if you have an area of your life that is in trouble, put God first in that area. If your marriage is in trouble, put God first. If your finances are in trouble, put God first. If you are in trouble, put God first.

That is the first step to problem solving: Put first things first. There is not a problem you face for which there is not a principle or a promise in God's Word that will get you through it.

Floods

So, the rains come, but then there are flood waters. Floods are next-level problems. Floods are a step up from rain problems. They are crises and emergencies like the loss of a loved one. Maybe you've gone through a divorce. Maybe you've lost a family member. Maybe you've had some sort of bad diagnosis in your body. It is a little more than just a rainy-day problem. It is a crisis in your life.

But, how you act or how you react is crucial. You can go through a storm and either break down or break through. You may do both, and that is okay. Sometimes you break down before you break through, but how you act in the storm is what brings you out on the other side.

When you go through a tragedy, you have got to take a couple of things away from it. Ask yourself, *What can I learn from this storm?* You can learn that God is in control.

Let me say it this way: Everything in your life is Father-filtered. I didn't say God brought it. I didn't say God caused it. I am just saying God is aware of it. God knows what you are going through. You are not out there alone. You have not been put on hold. God did not disconnect from you. God knows who you are. He knows what you are facing. He knows the size of the storm, and He is there waiting for you. God is in control.

You can also learn that God is your refuge. Psalms 46 says, "He is my strength and my refuge." When a storm comes and it is a significant one, what do you do? You go to your storm shelter. And here is the thing about a storm shelter: While you are in there, the storm is blowing through, and all Hell is breaking loose. You can hear it, and you know something is going on. But even in all of that, there is a certain peace on the inside that says, "I'm okay. I don't understand everything. I know things are going to be different. I know that at least right now when I am in this storm shelter, in this safe place, I am okay."

If you are in the middle of a flood, I'm sorry for what you are going through. But I'm going to tell you, if you will stay connected to God, you will be ok. You may lose some things, but if you've got God, you will get it back.

Wind

And that brings us to the last element, which is wind. I live in Oklahoma, which is Tornado Alley. We know that when a storm blows through, it looks different after the storm than it did before. When broadcasters interview people who have been through a tornado and have lost everything, you hear incredible statements like, "We still have each other."

They get it! I have even heard people whose houses have been demolished say, "There are people worse off than me." Are you kidding me?! What an attitude! That is an overcomer! Or you might hear them say things like this: "We will build it back."

That is how you face a storm. We know that with God, nothing is impossible. We know that even though the devil took it, God will give it back. We know that even though right now we are in a difficult situation, with God on our side, we will turn this thing around. The rain, floods, and winds may come, but you can learn that God is your refuge.

Then, after asking, *What can I learn?*, ask *What can I do?* The answer is to pray. Oftentimes, when we go through something, we have this attitude or this thought that says, "Well, the least we can do is pray about it."

It is not the least we can do! The *best* we can do is pray about it. Prayer works. God is a prayer-answering God. And when we pray, God answers.

The Bible says, "Call out to God or cast all of your cares on to God, because He cares for you (1 Peter 5:7)." And then Jesus goes on to give this incredible illustration. Jesus said, "Hold on just a minute.

Think about the birds of the air. They are pretty insignificant, but God takes care of them (Matthew 6:26-27)."

Can I ask you a question? Have you ever seen a worried bird? I mean seriously, have you ever seen a bird with ulcers or pacing back and forth saying, "What am I going to do?" God is going to take care of you. Understand that God has this and understands this. When you pray, you are praying to a God who never changes. Prayer works. The Bible says He is the same yesterday, today, and forever (Hebrews 13:8). And that just simply means whatever He has ever done for anyone, anywhere, He can do for you.

He loves you the same way that he loves Paul, Mary, and anyone that you have ever read about. He cares for us affectionately. We are praying to a God of wisdom. Someone once said that God is too loving to be cruel and too wise to make a mistake. I just have to trust Him.

When the wind blows through, things change. Some of you need to go with the change. Think of it this way: A friend of mine says, "You have already wasted too much time. You are not as young as you used to be, and you are not as young as you think you are."

Remember Acts chapter 27 from Chapter One of this book. Paul is on a ship. He is a prisoner, and they are taking him to prison. For 14 days, he has not seen the sun. For 14 nights, he has not seen the moon. He has been in a 14-day storm out on the ocean, a hurricane. Let's read:

Acts 27:9-18

Since much time had passed, and the voyage was now dangerous because even the Fast was already over, Paul advised them, saying, "Sirs, I perceive that the voyage will be with injury and much loss, not only of the cargo and the ship, but also of our lives." But the centurion paid more attention to the pilot and to the owner of the ship than to what Paul said. And because the harbor was not suitable to spend the winter in, the majority decided to put out to sea from there, on the chance that somehow they could reach Phoenix, a harbor of Crete, facing both southwest and northwest, and spend the winter there. Now when the south wind blew gently, supposing that they had obtained their purpose, they weighed anchor and sailed along Crete, close to the shore. But soon a tempestuous wind, called the northeaster, struck down from the land. And when the ship was caught and could not face the wind, we gave way to it and were driven along. Running under the lee of a small island called Cauda, we managed with difficulty to secure the ship's boat. After hoisting it up, they used supports to undergird the ship. Then, fearing that they would run aground on the Syrtis, they lowered the gear, and thus they were driven along. Since we were violently storm-tossed, they began the next day to jettison the cargo.

There are two things I want you to get out of that. The first is that before they ever went into the storm, Paul said, "I perceive something." Remember, one of the anchors that we have to get us through the storm is the supernatural. There is this whole invisible side of God that few Christians ever really tap into. There is a side of answered prayers, that when we fast, walls come down, and a side of angels and angelic activity all around us. There is this thing called the anointing of God, God's supernatural ability. All of this is available to us.

But most of us go through life never really tapping into the supernatural side of God. And what Paul is saying here is, "I perceive the Holy Spirit is showing me things."

I have often said there are things that you can know no other way than that the Holy Spirit is showing you. There is a supernatural side of life that we need to tune into. Paul said, "I don't know how I know it. I just know it. It is not a good thing. Let's not take this trip."

Then, Paul had a great big "I told you so". Have you ever had a bad idea? You just did something that was so stupid, and you thought, *Man! God was telling me all along not to do that, and I over-rode my conscience. I just ignored the council from the Word of God. I didn't listen to the Holy Spirit. Our lives would have been better if we would have just listened to what God said.*

Remember how I said that some storms are man made. Some people are storm chasers! They go looking for trouble.

Then in verse 18, here is one of the positive things about a storm that you may not realize at the time. It says they "lightened the ship". There is nothing like a storm to show you what is important or to reassess your values. That thing you thought was so important really does not matter anymore.

In the midst of the storm is this incredible opportunity to readjust our lives. What really counts? What really matters? What are the things that you want to live for? Is this what you want your legacy to be?

They do not build legacies and memorials to the great takers of the world. They build legacies to the great *givers* of the world, those who live for others. On my gravestone, I want two things: One is, "I told you I was sick." And then I want it to say what they said about David. "He served his generation well." *That* is a monument! *That* is a life!

Review

If you want to be able to withstand rain, floods, and winds, you must have a solid rock foundation. Jesus said that those who are doers of the Word and not just hearers only are the ones who will stand. Build your life on the foundation of God and His Word. Through an acronym of the word BUILD, we looked at the practical side of how to do that, live well, and end up leaving a strong legacy.

In the next chapter, we will focus on having a strong family, which flows from having a strong marriage. We will look at steps you can take for improving your marriage, and if you are not married, you can use them to give advice to people who are struggling in this area.

Take Action

1. Think about the parts of God's Word that you have not yet put into practice. Are you just a "hearer" or a "hearer and doer"?

_____

_____

_____

2. Write a description of the life you want. What distractions do you need to avoid to keep you on track?

_____

_____

_____

_____

_____

CHAPTER THREE

FAMILY DRAMA

A s I said in Chapter Two, this chapter is all about family drama. You might be able to relate. I want to begin by making a statement that both our marriages and our families are under attack spiritually. I am sure that some of you didn't just think, "Amen," but you thought, "That's me!"

Here is a cornerstone verse for this chapter and for your marriage. This is from Matthew chapter 19, verse six. It is very short and yet, very powerful:

Matthew 19:6

What God has joined together, let no man put asunder.

The word *asunder* means "to separate", and that really ought to be our challenge, our call, and our charge. Whatever God has joined together, let no man separate. That is pretty black and white; it is pretty definitive. And I could just dial that in a little bit more and say it this way: What that says to me is that your marriage is worth fighting for.

Your marriage is worth fighting for.

In fact, if you are married, you need to understand that your number one priority is your marriage relationship. Next to your relationship with God, it is your marriage. And our marriages should not take a back seat or low priority to anyone or anything. They have got to take first place in our lives. Your marriage does not just need *some* of your attention; it needs *most* of your attention.

Three Marriage Needs

There are three things that you need to continually have, or be doing, in and for your marriage.

Elevate

One of things that we need to constantly do is to elevate. Here is what I mean by that: We need to take our marriage and raise it above the fray of life. We need to raise it above mediocrity. We need to keep our marriage up out of the toxins of this world.

Life, in general, becomes busy, and our marriages can become mediocre or can become a part of the busyness of life if we are not careful. We need to make sure that we never let that happen to our marriages. We need to keep them elevated so that we can see them and keep them raised up above the fray of busyness, toxins or mediocrity.

Celebrate

The second thing we need to do is to celebrate, because marriages can become very predictable, and oftentimes, when something goes well in your marriage, you need to take that moment and celebrate it, because if you spend all of your time focusing on the things that are wrong, you are going to miss all of the things that are going great.

If, however, you take every little thing and turn it into a victory, you are going to find yourself not complaining about your marriage, but celebrating how good life is together. The day-to-day victories, good moments, and memories need to be celebrated.

Educate

We are going to elevate, celebrate, and then third, we need to educate ourselves concerning marriage. Whatever occupation you are in, that occupation changes simply because of time. There are technology updates, and there are times and seasons. For you to stay on your "A game", you have got to be constantly learning and relearning your trade. You have to constantly keep up with the changes that are taking place in the market.

Marriages are the same way. There are seasons and life changes. As you get older in marriage, you are in different seasons. You should always be aware of the one you are in and educate yourself.

We know that it is true that leaders really are readers. And husbands, if you are going to lead your marriage, you need to be reading about what a marriage should be. You need to be gaining techniques, understanding things from the Word of God, and reading things from books and articles that say, "This will make my marriage better," or, "That will make me a better husband."

Fight for Your Family

The devil hates your marriage. In fact, the devil hates anything that has to do with family. In a book called *Real Marriage*, the author makes the statement, "Satan didn't even show up on planet Earth until after Adam and Eve were married[3]."

I think of it this way: The moment Satan saw a marriage on planet Earth, he moved in to separate Adam and Eve from God and to divide them from one another. Satan hates marriage, and to make it personal, he hates *your* marriage. He hates your home. He hates your life. He hates your kids. He hates your dog. He hates your cat...

Satan hates anything and everything that has to do with your life and your marriage relationship, and he is going to do anything he can to destroy it. That is why you have to make the decision to fight for your family.

If your marriage is struggling, it will not automatically get better. If you say, "I am going to let time pass, and we will let some things roll on. Maybe this will shake itself out; maybe my marriage will get better," it is just not going to happen. You have to chart a course and make a plan in order to have a better marriage relationship.

I want to try to reshape your idea, or ideology, of marriage. The purpose of marriage is not to live happily ever after.

Now, I know what you're thinking. *What?! The purpose of marriage is not to live happily ever after?!* Listen, all of those fairy tales, all of those shows on the *Hallmark Channel,* all of those romantic movies that are telling you that you get married and live happily ever after have all lied to you. The purpose of marriage is *not* to make you happy. And because we think the purpose is to make us happy, we end up putting happiness at the center of our marriage relationship.

When you put happiness at the center, or the focal point, of a relationship, it creates a lot of family drama. Let me say it this way: Happiness is not a good way to measure the health of your marriage.

Now, don't misunderstand me. God does not want you to be miserable or to have a miserable marriage. God doesn't want you to be *un*happy. But here is the problem: Happiness and love are not the same thing, not by a long shot...not even close. Here is why: To really love someone, you are often going to have to override your own happiness. Happiness is about *me*, but love is when I place *you* above myself. That is what marriage is.

Marriage is when you find somebody in life, and you say, "I am willing to place that person in front of myself and his or her needs in front of my needs." If you are not willing or ready to do that, you are not ready to be married. Until you look at someone and say, "My goal in life is to fulfill your happiness," you are not ready to be married.

Here is the formula: Put love before happiness, and oftentimes (in fact, most times), happiness comes. But if you get happiness before love, it is never going to be successful. So marriage is not to make *you* happy; marriage is for you to make *someone else* happy.

One author said this: "Marriage is not about happiness; it is about holiness. God uses marriage to draw you closer to Him[4]." Marriage will make you pray. Marriage will make you cry out to God and seek His face.

Five Action Steps for Improving Your Marriage

I want to give you five action steps for having a better marriage, and I want this to be a rubber-meets-the-road type of lesson. These are not just some good ideas, but some action steps that you can actually put into practice.

Action Step 1: Put on Rose-Colored Glasses

When you put on rose-colored glasses, everywhere you look and everything you see looks rosy, because you are choosing to view life through that filter. You are focusing on what is *right* with your marriage and spouse rather than what is *wrong* with your marriage and spouse.

If you put any one of us under a microscope, you are going to find some flaws. None of us can withstand the microscope, so we have to be willing to put on rose-colored glasses and be willing to accept some things and believe the best about our spouse. If you have ever heard the prayer of Saint Francis of Assisi, it is really a great prayer for marriage.

It says, "Lord, teach me to accept the things I cannot change. Give me the courage to change the things I can, and the wisdom to know the difference."

Accept

Those three words (accept, courage, and wisdom) go a long way to building a solid marriage foundation. Let's look at the word *accept* for just a moment. There are certain things in a marriage relationship you are just going to have to accept and say, "It is what it is. That is the way things are." You are going to have to learn to accept and perhaps appreciate those annoying things that your spouse does.

You might say, "Pastor, you don't understand. He clips his toenails at the table!" Well, at least he clips his toenails! You don't want to be sleeping with Edward Scissorhands, right? "But Pastor, she never cleans her hair out of the drain!" Well, at least she does shower regularly.

You know what I'm talking about. You've got to choose to see your spouse in the best light, and you've got to accept those things that are annoyances and turn them around, because honestly, you are pretty annoying yourself.

Courage

The word *courage* is important for a marriage because marriage is not for the faint of heart. It takes courage to get married and to stay married. It takes courage to fight against the odds.

Wisdom

And then it takes wisdom. One of the words translated *wisdom* in the Hebrew is the word *skill*. It takes skill to build a successful marriage. That is why I said you need to educate yourself and read to get better at it.

Action Step 2: Empty the Drama Box

The second thing that you need to do in a marriage relationship is to empty out the drama box. Let me explain what that means.

Here is the problem with marriage: Oftentimes we look at marriage, and we think that all of our marriage problems are external. We say, "He's fat," or "She's ugly," or "Too much sex and not enough money," or "Too much money and not enough sex..." and all of this stuff.

We do not communicate. We think, *My spouse is not fun anymore...* He says, "She's got too many problems; too much baggage..." You see all of these things, and you think, *Man! Marriage is rotten!*

But most of the problems in marriage are not external; they are *internal*. Let me illustrate what I mean by the drama box. I am sure you have a junk drawer at home. You know what I'm talking about. Some of you may have graduated from the drawer to a closet. The garage is next.

If we could take an inner picture of you, it would be like a junk box. And in this box is all of your emotions (the good, the bad, the ugly), all of your pain and all of your frustration, all of the things that you are going through, all of your ideas, your wrong thinking, your hang ups, and your disappointments.

All of us have stuff on the inside, and when we come to the idea that we believe that our marriage problems are external, we look at all of that stuff and that thing that he is or she is or what you don't like, and you just say, "I am walking away from that mess."

But your junk box goes with you. All you have done is walk away from the clutter of marriage. Have you ever heard the saying, "No matter where you go, there you are"? You cannot run from yourself. You think you are leaving that stuff, and yet, you take all of your problems, all of your issues, all of your struggles with you. You drag them right into the next relationship.

What you have to do is learn to deal with the issues in the box. You have got to clean out the junk drawer. And you might ask, "Well, how do I do that?"

It's messy, like sorting the laundry. You take one issue at a time. You bring it to God and you say, "God, I need healing over this issue. God, I need to give it to you. I am bringing it to you because I can't handle it. I don't know what to do with it."

One by one, you take the issues, the hang ups, the hurts, the problems, and you bring them to God for healing, because remember; He is a healing God. He is a healer from the inside out. You bring it to God and lift it up. You sincerely lay it before Him and say, "God, I give this to you. I can't deal with it. I can't handle it. But I know that you are the God of everything, the Lord of my marriage and the God of everything in my life. I am asking you to bring healing in this area of my life."

I am telling you; He will do it. But you have to empty out the junk drawer. Marriage will never get better if you just change the external things and you don't change the internal things that need to happen in your life. James chapter four, verse one says:

James 4:1

What causes fights and quarrels among you? Don't they come from the desires that battle within you?

Most of our marriage problems are not external; they are internal.

Action Step 3: Communication

Number three is a great action step: Communication. You can start on that today. Ephesians 4:29 says:

Ephesians 4:29

Let no corrupt communication proceed out of your mouth, but only that which is good for the purpose of edifying, that it may minister grace.

When you boil it down, here is what that verse is literally saying: "Don't say rotten, ugly things." Don't let those things come out of your mouth and into your marriage relationship, because here is the thing about words: Words can't be taken back once they are out there.

Have you ever said something, and the moment you said it, you thought, *I wish I wouldn't have said that?* You almost physically just want to reach out and try to grab those words before they get to the ear of the hearer.

I think of it like locking your keys in your car. The moment you shut the door, you instantly remember, "Oh no! My keys are in there! I can't believe I just did that! This is going to cost me time and money."

Don't say rotten, ugly things. Proverbs 18:21 is a verse that I love. It says:

Proverbs 18:21

The tongue has the power of life and death, and those who love it will eat its fruit.

In other words, our words can either hurt or heal. They can create a war, or they can bring peace in our situation. James chapter three says, "If you control your tongue, then you are perfect." The word *perfect* here means mature and healthy. What he is saying is, the only way to have a healthy marriage relationship is when you control your words. Words create a healthy marriage.

Here is another thing that communication does: Communication narrows the gap between you and your spouse. If there is a gap, if there is a chasm between you, you have to begin to talk through that thing. The more you begin to talk, the smaller that chasm, or gap, will become through communication.

Communication draws you closer to your spouse. We create the world that we live in by the words that come out of our mouth. When God created the heavens and the earth, when God created the world, He *spoke* it into existence. By speaking, He created this incredible world that we live in.

We create our own world that we live in by what we say. If you want to change the world you live in, you have got to change the things that you say. Speak life into your marriage relationship.

Action Step 4: Show Affection

Step four is to show affection. Affection in a marriage is a big deal. It is a bond. It is a cohesion, of sorts. In fact, let me say it in a way that we can remember: It is glue for the two of you. It keeps you glued together.

So the question is, if you have lost that loving feeling, how do you rekindle the love? There is a great verse out of the book of Revelation that is helpful for our marriages. I know when you think about Revelation, you don't normally think about marriage, but this one is a great verse: Revelation 2:4-5. This is Jesus talking to the church.

Revelation 2:4-5

The love you had at first is gone. Remember how far you've fallen. Return to me. Change the way you think and act, and do what you did at first.

There are four things in this verse that we can use to resurrect a marriage relationship.

Remember

The first thing that Jesus said was, "Remember..." I'm going to challenge you to think back for a moment and to remember why you wanted to marry your spouse in the first place. I mean, there was something there. There was a time when you saw him or her, and you were so drawn to that you said, "I want to spend my life with this person."

Maybe it was their smile. Maybe it was their personality. Maybe it was just their outlook on life. Whatever it was, you saw something in them, and you said, "I want to be around that. I like that. I want that in my life." I promise you, that is still there. Find that spark, and remember what brought you together to start with.

Return

And then Jesus said, "Return..." Return to your love. Give your spouse your whole heart and commitment. It is a decision that says, "I made a vow. I made a commitment. We said some things before God, and it was not just a ceremony; it was a covenant that we drew up with God. And those things that I said in the sight of God, I made a solemn oath for better, for worse, for richer, for poorer, and I am going to be a person of my word."

Repent

And then Jesus told the church, "You need to repent." Repentance is not just an apology. Apologies are good and necessary, but let me just say this: If you cannot say, "I'm sorry," you are not ready to get married. If you cannot say, "I was wrong," you are too immature to be married, because a marriage relationship is filled with "I'm sorrys" and "I was wrongs".

Oftentimes, when I teach on marriage, one of the things that I do is have couples stand. I tell the husband and wives to look at each other. I look at the husbands and say, "Because you are the leader of the home, I want you to look at your wife and say, 'I'm sorry. I was wrong. Please forgive me.'" They do that, and there is a lot of uneasy laughter.

Then I say, "Okay, that was the trial run. Let's do it for real now. Husbands, look at your wives and say, 'I'm sorry. I was wrong. Please forgive me.'" Next I say, "Wives, look at your husband and say, 'I do forgive you. I'm sorry, and I love you.'"

Every time I have ever done that, I have seen tears flowing down the faces of husbands and wives, because sometimes there is an incredible barrier that says, "I can't until she does this or he does that." Sometimes they think, *I can't say that. I don't know what to say.* Sometimes the only thing you need to say is just, "I'm sorry."

Repenting is not just an apology. It is deeper than that. And then repeat. That means just keep doing steps one through three as often as you need to, over and over and over, because it is a healing formula.

Action Step 5: Make God a Partner

Action step number five is, you have to make God a partner in your marriage. A successful marriage does not just consist of a husband and wife, but it is between three: a husband, a wife, and God. Ecclesiastes 4:12 says that a three-stranded cord is not easily broken. God is that third strand. God is that securing strand of a marriage relationship, meaning that a marriage that has God at the center of it has a much greater chance of succeeding than a marriage without Him.

What I am saying is that God wants to be a partner in your marriage, and He does not want to be a silent partner. He wants to have a voice in your marriage.

When I say, "Make God a partner," that happens on two levels. If you have never made Jesus Christ the Lord of your life and you are working on your marriage, the greatest thing you can do is to make Jesus the Lord of your life. I cannot tell you the healing that would bring in a marriage relationship. When you both make God a partner, then you two have something in common.

Even if you have already made Jesus the Lord of your life, there are times when you need to re-dedicate your life and say, "God, I have got my life uncalibrated. I need you to recalibrate my life. I have lost my true north, and I need you to get me back on the right path. So today, I rededicate my life to you." Not only does it help you, but it heals your marriage.

Then, we need to invite God into our marriage, saying, "Jesus, you are Lord of this marriage." That means we are not taking the advice of every person around us. We are going to do what the Word says. "Jesus, you are the Lord of this marriage, and so therefore, I am not going to live my marriage the way the world does and act like the world does. I am going to build it up according to the Word of God."

We invite God into our lives on a personal level, and we invite Him into our marriage relationship, meaning that we let Him lead. Seek Him first, and follow His plan.

Realize that God created marriage. It is a God thing. It was His idea. And since it was His idea, He knows how it works, and He knows how to heal it. He knows how to give you patience. He is your source of love, and He can give your marriage resurrection power. Sometimes our marriages need a resurrection in some area.

Marriage is not always easy, but it is one of the most rewarding things. Marriage is not here to make us happy; it is here to make us holy. Marriage is here so that we can love someone else unconditionally with the love of God.

Review

Are you fighting for your marriage? Are you always thinking about how you can improve it? In this chapter, we talked about how your marriage needs to be elevated and celebrated, and how you need to always be educate yourself about it. Marriage is a skill, and as with any skill, it takes knowledge and practice of fundamental principles to be good at it. Practice the action steps I gave, and don't give up. God can help you restore a broken marriage.

In the next chapter, we will look at how to weather financial storms that come our way and how to prevent some of them. God has a lot in His Word to say about how we manage money, and we will examine some verses for guidance.

Take Action

1. How can you do a better job at elevating your spouse?

   _____

   _____

   _____

2. How you can put God more at the center of your marriage.

   _____

   _____

   _____

CHAPTER FOUR

FINANCIAL STORMS

T here is a temptation when we find ourselves in the middle of a financial storm to forget certain Bible principles. Sometimes we just throw our hands up in the air, and out of frustration, we go deeper into debt or even blame God because of our circumstances.

But whatever the cause of your financial storm (if it's just too much debt to manage, or maybe there has been a loss of a job or health issues), you have to keep hoping and believing for a better future. In other words, do not blame God for where you are. Trust God, and believe Him to lead you into a better future.

The Bible says that we walk by faith, and that should tell you something right there. We do not look at our situations and circumstances in an ordinary way, but we look at our situations through the filter of faith. That means we are not moved by what we see, by what we hear, or by natural circumstances; we are moved by faith to do something according to the Word of God.

Now, when I say to live by faith, do not take the attitude that says, "Pastor, I tried living by faith once." Well, that is not how it works. It is a continual thing.

The Bible says that faith is a *lifestyle*. A friend of mine used to say it this way: "When it comes to issues or troubles in people's lives, too many of them just want to shack up with Jesus until the need is over."

In other words, when there is a need they say, "I just want to get in, get what I need, and then get back out again. Thank you very much, Jesus. I am glad you were there for me." But that is not what the Bible teaches. Romans 1:17 says that the just shall live by faith, meaning that faith is an ongoing lifestyle.

Now, there is another thing to add. Most of the blessings of God are conditional, and the condition to every blessing of God is faith. A lot of people will say, "I am living by faith," but let me show you a picture of what that looks like, because I'm not sure everybody who says, "I'm in faith" really understand what faith is.

First of all, when I am walking by faith, I am going to spend more time praising God than complaining about my life. That is what a faith lifestyle looks like. -not just coming to God and telling Him all about my troubles, but coming to God and in faith, inviting Him into my circumstances.

Walking by faith means my prayers are filled with faith and not fear. They are faith-fueled prayers, speaking God's Word over my life and into my circumstances. Walking by faith means that I am confident that at the end of the day, no matter how it looks right now, when it is all said and done, with God's help, I am going to come out on top.

We are not just *saying* that, but we *know* that. "It may look bad, but when it is all said and done, I know that God is going to promote me out of this thing." That is walking by faith. Walking by faith is when I am focused on Heaven and not on Earth, when I am more aware of what God says than what my circumstance is.

Let me add to never forget that God does not move because of crisis. God does not move because of panic. God does not move because of desperation. God moves according to faith.

Now, here are a couple of verses that I think every Christian ought to have highlighted in his or her Bible, dog-eared, or marked somewhere on a device. You should read them over and over. One is Matthew 19:26. It is very simple and yet very powerful.

Matthew 19:26

But with God, all things are possible.

"But with God..." That *but* says that whatever came before that is negated. With God, all things are possible. The next verse, which is Mark 9:23 says:

Mark 9:23

All things are possible to Him that believes.

Those are two verses that motivate and inspire me, that challenge me to live my life by faith. Now, one of the names of God is the name Jehovah Jireh, which translated means "the Lord is my provider". Let me give you the history behind that name.

In Genesis chapter two, God dealt with Abraham, the father of our faith, and God used him. Abraham is the father of faith because of his obedience. God said, "Abraham, I want you to take your son, Isaac, and I want you to sacrifice him." Remember, the Old Testament was blood and guts; The New Testament is grace and glory. Thank

God we are born in this dispensation! And so God said, "I want you to make a sacrifice, but I am going to ask you to sacrifice your son."

The promise God made to Abraham, his son Isaac, represented his future. He represented everything that God had said, every promise. "I want you to lay Isaac on the altar and trust me completely." So, Abraham took his son and laid him on the altar.

He was getting ready to sacrifice him in obedience to God. He raised his hand with the knife, when an audible voice from Heaven said, "Stop! Don't do this!" God stopped him, and then He said, "I want you to look around (because there was still a sacrifice that needed to happen), and nearby, stuck by its horns in a bush was a big ram. God said, "There is your sacrifice."

Here is the thing about God, and especially financially: God is never late, but He is usually not early either. And so Abraham looked at the sacrifice, and he said, "Jehovah Jireh, My God Provides!" That is a name that God reveals Himself by. He is saying that He is our source.

I want you to realize, your job is not your source; God is. God has given you your job. God gives you the strength to go to your job. God gives you the wisdom and talent to carry out your job. But your job is not your source; God is. Your parents are not your source, so it is okay to go ahead and move out of the basement. You can trust God. He will get you through this. The government is also not your source; God is. Let me connect that thought with this verse:

Psalm 8:4

What is man that you God are mindful of him and the son of man that you have visited him?

Who is this man? Who is this creation that you know who he is and are mindful of him? This incredible God that created this universe knows *who* you are, *where* you are, *what* you need, and *how* to get it to you. The Bible says that He has a plan for your life, and part of that plan is to prosper you.

I want to give more Scripture verses to you and get our focus on the goodness of God and His nature. This is what I call a "feel good moment". This feel good moment is brought to you by the King James Version. Enjoy.

Philippians 4:19

My God shall supply all of your needs according to his riches and glory through Christ Jesus.

Isaiah 1:19

If you are willing and obedient, you shall eat of the good of the land.

Proverbs 10:22

The blessing of the Lord brings wealth and adds no sorrow to it.

3 John 2

I pray above all things that you may prosper and be in health even as your knowledge of the Word of God grows.

Deuteronomy 8:18

It is the Lord God who gives you power to get well.

Psalm 3:5-7

The Lord takes pleasure in the prosperity of his servants.

Psalms 37:25

I have never seen the righteous forsaken or his seed begging for bread.

Joshua 1:8

God will make your way prosperous.

Those verses and many, many more just like them are painting a picture. Does that sound like a God who wants to keep you down, hold you back, or punish you? To me, that sounds like a God who is for you, wants to promote you, and wants to see you to succeed in life.

Master Your Money

I want to give you some principles from the Bible that will help you to experience the blessings of God. The first one is: Master your money. If you do not master money, money will master you. Do you remember the story of the rich young ruler? This comes out of Matthew's Gospel. Jesus encountered this guy, and it says:

Matthew 19:16-21

And behold, a man came up to him, saying, "Teacher, what good deed must I do to have eternal life?" And he said to him, "Why do you ask me about what is good? There is only one who is good. If you would enter life, keep the commandments." He said to him, "Which ones?" And Jesus said, "You shall not murder, You shall not commit adultery, You shall not steal, You shall not bear false witness, Honor your father and mother, and, You shall love your neighbor as yourself." The young man said to him, "All these I have kept. What do I still lack?" Jesus said to him, "If you would be perfect, go, sell what you possess and give to the poor, and you will have treasure in heaven; and come, follow me."

Jesus did not tell everyone He encountered to follow Him. In fact, most of the time, Jesus told people, "Don't follow me. Go back home. Tell your tribe. Tell your people what I am all about, but do not follow me."

There were a certain select few to whom He said, "I want you to follow me." Was He perhaps calling this man to be a Judas replacement? Remember Judas, who denied Christ? Had this guy followed God and had he been able to manage money, we might be reading today the Gospel according to the rich young ruler. Who knows?

When the young man heard this, he went away sad, because he had great wealth (or great wealth had him). Then, Jesus said to his disciples, "Truly, I tell you, it is hard for someone who is rich to enter the Kingdom of Heaven. It is easier for a camel to go through the eye of a needle." And He is not talking about people with possessions not being able to get into Heaven. He is talking about not being able to manage your money.

There are so many lessons in this story, but let me focus on one aspect. The rich young ruler could not follow God because he couldn't master his money. Let me say it this way: Because he was mastered *by* his money, he could not follow the Master. Money is a spiritual matter, and it will either make you God's tool or Satan's fool.

There are some 500 verses in the New Testament on the subject of prayer and 400 plus verses on faith. But there are over 2,000 verses on managing your possessions. Of the 38 parables Jesus taught, 16 of them dealt with money management: how to handle your money and how to deal with possessions once you have them. What Jesus is saying is, how you handle money or how you manage your money, is a gauge of your spirituality.

Now, don't get mad at me; I am telling you the truth. But do not tell me how spiritually deep you are if you are not a giver. Don't try to impress me with your knowledge of Scripture if you are not a giver, because giving is a heart issue. Until you learn to become a giver in the things of God, you have not reached spirituality. 2 Corinthians 9:6 says:

2 Corinthians 9:6

Whoever sows sparingly will also reap sparingly, and whoever sows generously will reap generously.

Now, it is really easy to read over that verse and miss what He is really saying. What is He saying? He is saying this: Prosperity is a choice. Blessings are a choice. How do you receive the abundance of God? You receive God's abundance by making good choices. Here is a good choice: Choose not to serve money. Ecclesiastes 5:15 says:

Ecclesiastes 5:15

As he came from his mother's womb, naked shall he return. He shall carry nothing away in his hand.

You came into this world with nothing. You are going to leave this world with nothing. Do you realize that money cannot be taken to Heaven or to Hell? Money in this world is like money in a Monopoly game. It is good as long as you are sitting at the table. But once you get up from the table and walk away, it is no good whatsoever. The money that you have in this life is only good while you are here.

The more money you have in this life simply means the more money you are going to leave behind. I love the statement Rick Warren made. "It is not a sin to have money, but it is a sin to die rich." Here is another one. He said, "Do your giving while you're living, so you're knowing where it's going[6]."

Become a Child of God

Next, if you want to experience God's blessings on your life, become a child of God. We are not all God's children. We are all God's creation, but only those who have made Jesus Christ the Lord of their life are a son or daughter of God.

Jesus looked at a group of people, a bunch of Pharisees, and He said, "You are of your father, the devil." So, not everybody who is created is a child of God, but once you make Jesus Christ the Lord of your life, you can expect to experience the blessings of God.

When you become a child of God, you place yourself under the care of the good shepherd. Remember the 23rd Psalm. The Lord is my shepherd. I shall not want. He leads me, guides me, takes care of me and protects me. Even when my enemies surround me, goodness and mercy follow and pursue me. The blessings of God overtake me. That is all in the 23rd Psalm.

What he's saying is that the skill of the shepherd determines the health and success of the sheep. When you submit your life to God and make Jesus the Lord of your life, He guides you into abundant life.

Put God First

Number three: Put God first. I have often said that if there is any area of your life that you are struggling in, if there is any area of your life that is not working out for you or that you are not having success in, go back and put God first in that area. Make Jesus the Lord over that area of your life. And if you are facing a financial storm, put God first financially.

Here is the thing when it comes to finances: It is easy to push God to the back of the line. It is easy to put God on the back burner. This is because God does not auto-draft. God does not send you a bill, and He is not in your face about it. But God *does* say in the act of giving and tithing, to put Him first.

Tithing, or giving, is an act of worship. It is not buying God off, and it is not trying to buy His blessings. It is an act of obedience and an act of worship. What I am sharing is to try to help you, so don't get upset.

It is kind of like if you were to go to the dentist with a tooth that is hurting, and the dentist said, "I know this is hurting, so I am not going to touch it. I know the source of your pain, but I am not about to touch it because you are going to get mad at me." Malachi 3:10 says:

Malachi 3:8-12

"But you ask, 'How are we robbing you?'"In tithes and offerings. You are under a curse—your whole nation—because you are robbing me. Bring the whole tithe into the storehouse, that there may be food in my house. Test me in this," says the Lord Almighty, "and see if I will not throw open the floodgates of heaven and pour out so much blessing that there will not be room enough to store it. I will prevent pests from devouring your crops, and the vines in your fields will not drop their fruit before it is ripe," says the Lord Almighty. "Then all the nations will call you blessed, for yours will be a delightful land," says the Lord Almighty.

So what it is saying in this verse is that tithing is 10% of your income right up front. You bring it to God, and it brings the blessing of God. I know there are people who will say, "Well Pastor, I have never tithed, and I've done all right." Well, that was yesterday when you did it out of ignorance, but tomorrow, you will be doing it out of rebellion.

Let me give you an illustration. I am going to show you how tithing works. Tithing means that if I make a dollar, 10 cents belongs to God. Out of every $10 I make, $1 belongs to God. Out of every $100 I make, $10 belongs to God. I am going to show you how grace-filled, great, and gracious God is in our lives.

Pretend I have 10 loaves of bread, and God says, "All right, here is how this works: One loaf right off the top is mine. The other nine are yours. And I want to remind you what the one loaf is for. It is for taking Jesus to others, reaching the world, and telling the greatest story ever told so that there will be ministry in my house and so that the local church will stay strong. This is for helping people to get their hearts healed and their lives put back together. This one is mine. Those nine are yours. Take yours. Live a blessed life. Have a good life. Pay your bills, build your future, and build your dream house. Take care of your kids. Have fun. Do whatever you want to do. Nine are yours; one is mine.

But what happens is, we say, "Whoa! Slow down, God! Hold on just a moment. We need to negotiate. In fact, I am going to need to hold on to yours for just a little while here."

And God says, "Well, wait a minute. Let me remind you. Nine are yours. One is mine. You take nine and you live off of it. You do what you want to do. Make your dreams come true. Live a blessed life. But one is for *others*. One is for taking this incredible, life-changing, life-altering message of Jesus into the lives of other people, into your community, into mission fields around the world: feeding the hungry, clothing the poor, building missionary churches... all of these things. One is mine."

And we end up saying, "God, you don't understand. I am going to need yours, too." And we paint this picture of greed like a dog guarding a bone. "Don't even reach for it, God. Don't even think about it. This is mine!" What kind of picture is that? That is not the type of person I want to be. That is not the picture I want painted of my life. Tithing is a declaration that you are trusting in God's economy and not man's.

Now, when you tithe, your money never leaves you. It goes to God. God blesses it, multiplies it, and sends it back to you with more. And that ought to change your whole concept of giving. It never goes away. That is what I call a win-win. It is a win-win because I am being obedient to God. I am getting the abundance of God, and on top of that, when you give to God through the church, you are blessing the church.

And there is no other organization that does what we do. We deal with eternity. Wal-Mart and Chick-fil-a do not deal with eternity. We do. We eternally change lives, heal the hearts of hurting people, and give hope and courage to those who need it. We help to restore marriages, build leaders, reach the lost, and take Jesus into other countries. We feed the poor and build churches. So, giving to God is a win-win situation.

Pray for God's Help

Number four: Pray for God's help to get out of debt. In 2 Kings 6, we read that there was a Bible school in the Old Testament called the School of the Prophets. It was an Old Testament school, and Elisha was the teacher (I would like to go to that Bible school). They were building the school and building houses. They borrowed an axe head made out of iron, and those were very expensive and hard to come by. They did not have one, so they borrowed one.

While one of the students was chopping down trees to build the Bible school, the axe head came off the handle and fell into the river. Because it was borrowed, because it was precious, because you could not just run down to Methuselah's hardware store and get another one, it is a picture of debt. Now they owed something. How were they going to repay this? They were in a bad debt situation.

So what do they do? They tell Elisha, and he prays. He asks for God's favor, and what happens next is a miracle. The iron axe head floats to the top! The students reach in, grab it, and go back to work. That is a picture of asking God's blessing on your debt and God supernaturally coming through and helping. It was a supernatural debt reduction.

You can invite God into your debt, even if you created it. You can say, "God, forgive me, but please help me to get out of this. I need your blessing not only on my giving, but on supernatural debt cancellation." A lady once told me she had thousands and thousands of dollars in credit card debt.

Do you know the principle of the hole? When you find yourself in a hole, quit digging. I think credit cards ought to come with a warning, just like a pack of cigarettes. *The surgeon general has determined that smoking may be hazardous to your health.* Credit cards need to come with a warning. "Using this card is going to affect your health. It is going to rob you of your joy. It can cause divorce. It is going to put you in bondage. Before you use it, think twice." I think that would be good advice.

But she said, "All of these thousands and thousands of dollars of debt that I owed, I took it to God, and God supernaturally walked me out of it." Take that principle, and you can believe God for supernatural debt reduction in your life.

Sow a Seed

Number five: Sow a seed. In everything that God does in our lives, God has a part to play, and we have a part to play. We are partnering with God, and we are doing this together. In other words, it would be wrong to say, "God, I invite you in and ask you to do your part, but I am not willing to do my part." Maybe your part is to sow a seed. Luke 6:38 says this:

Luke 6:38

Give, and it will be given to you. A good measure, pressed down, shaken together and running over, will be poured into your lap. For with the measure you use, it will be measured to you.

Now, if you want a small harvest, sow a small seed. If you want little increase, give a little offering. God is saying, "If you give to me with your smallest measure, when I give back to you, I am going to give back with my smallest measure." Do you want to know why God does that? It is because He loves you.

He is giving back to you according to your ability to handle and understand money. Let me say it this way: You do not give car keys to a first grader, because he is going to hurt someone. The worst whipping I ever got was in the first grade. I took my mom's car keys out of her purse, drove the car into the basketball goal, and crumpled it over the top of the car.

As I was still trying to figure out what was going on, I looked out the window, and my dad had the car door handle in one hand and his belt in the other. I was like a monkey trying to slap that lock down, but I just could not do it fast enough. You do not give the car keys to a first grader, but when we come to the place where we say, "God, I can trust you," God begins to put His blessing on your life. When I do my part, God does His part.

Review

Financial storms are nothing to laugh about. They are difficult and sometimes overwhelming. That is why I am sharing these principles. I want you to walk in God's abundance. Do not blame God. He is never the problem; He is always the answer. Trust that He can change your future, and let Him help you change some habits that might need changing.

If you tend to be someone who lives a life of worry, the next chapter is for you. God has made some promises that we can cling to. We will walk through those, as well as some practical steps to help you overcome worry.

Take Action

1. If you are in debt, pray for God to teach you how to get out. Pray for Him to give you the self disciple necessary to get out.

2. If you are not a natural, joyful giver, practice giving regularly, and see how God can use that to change your heart. Where could you start?

_____

_____

_____

CHAPTER FIVE

WIN OVER WORRY

I want to begin with a question. When it comes to worry, would you say you have a master's degree? I mean, if worry were an Olympic event, would you win the gold? Maybe we can dial that in a little bit and ask, do you worry more than you should? I think we all are prone to it. It is something we have got to constantly work with and guard against.

Let me set the foundation by telling you what Jesus said to people when they were worried. He said five things. First, He said, "Fear not." That is good advice. When you are worried and concerned about things, don't let fear take over. He said, "Trust God," and then, "Don't be anxious." Do not let those emotions rise up on the inside of you. He said," Don't let your mind go wild," and then just, "Don't worry." That is maybe one of the most powerful messages that Jesus taught in his ministry. So the question is, why should you not worry?

Why Not Worry?

Let me give you four reasons that I think are very valid as to why you should not worry. Here is number one:

God is on Your Side

If God is for you, who can be against you (Romans 8:31)? This is not just for hype. It is a Bible reality that God is on your side. And if God is on your side, you are on the winning team.

God Will Never Leave You, nor Forsake You

Number two: God said, "I will never leave you, nor forsake you (Hebrews 13:5)." No matter what you are going through, God is with you always.

The Power of God is Always the Same

Then I would tell you that the power of God is the same yesterday, today, and forever (Hebrews 13:8). That just simply means that whatever God has ever done for anyone, He can, through faith, do for you today. God is willing and ready to work on your behalf.

God is a Miracle-Working God

When you think about it, we have a God who can do anything but fail. If you do not get any further, understand this: God is, was, and always will be a miracle-working God. God is not ready to retire. He is not slowing down, aging out, losing His memory, or looking for a change. God is God, and He has not changed. He is still the same God from the Old Testament to the New Testament.

Let me tell you what worry really is. It is sin. I hope that just hit you in the face to realize what we have been doing is a sin. Here is why: When I worry, it is my way of saying, "God, I don't trust you." Worry is distrusting God and being aggravated at Him. It is saying, "God, you don't care. If you did care, I wouldn't be going through this. God, I'm not looking to you to get me through this, and I'm really a little bit upset that you're not moving more in my life."

Worry is sin. Listen to what Jesus said concerning worry. In Matthew chapters five, six, and seven, Jesus is doing an incredible amount of preaching, and He deals with the subject of worry that we all face. Not much has changed. Here is what He said:

Matthew 6:25-34

Therefore I tell you, do not be anxious about your life, what you will eat or what you will drink, nor about your body, what you will put on. Is not life more than food, and the body more than clothing? Look at the birds of the air: they neither sow nor reap nor gather into barns, and yet your heavenly Father feeds them. Are you not of more value than they? And which of you by being anxious can add a single hour to his span of life? And why are you anxious about clothing? Consider the lilies of the field, how they grow: they neither toil nor spin, yet I tell you, even Solomon in all his glory was not arrayed like one of these. But if God so clothes the grass of the field, which today is alive and tomorrow is thrown into the oven, will he not much more clothe you, O you of little faith? Therefore do not be anxious, saying, 'What shall we eat?' or 'What shall we drink?' or 'What shall we wear?' For the Gentiles seek after all these things, and your heavenly Father knows that you need them all. But seek first the kingdom of God and his righteousness, and all these things will be added to you." Therefore do not be anxious about tomor-

row, for tomorrow will be anxious for itself. Sufficient for
the day is its own trouble.

That is Jesus' way of saying that you cannot change anything
or improve anything through worry. Jesus is saying over and over in
this message, "Don't be afraid. Don't worry." In fact, five times in
those verses He says, "Take no thought about your life." Don't get focused on and build these things up in your mind. He said, "Don't be
anxious. Don't let emotions overtake you."

Do you think that maybe He is trying to tell us something?
Here is what studies have shown us about worry: 85% of the things
that we worry about never happen. That same study showed that out of
500 people, when something *did* happen, 79% of those people in the
study were able to handle that problem much better than they thought
they would be able to.[7] In other words, they found strength and the
ability to get through what they thought was going to be an impossible
situation.

There was another study that revealed that 92% of our emotional energy is spent worrying about things that either will not happen
or that we cannot change. That is why some of you are so worn out, so
tired, and so emotionally distraught. You have been putting all of your
emotional energy into worrying, but worry cannot change anything.

What You Should Do About Worry

I love the example of Paul in the book of Acts. Do you remember when he built the fire and a snake came out? He reached in,
and a snake fastened to his arm. Do you know what Paul did? He
shook it off. He didn't start a worriers' club. He didn't start a worry

connect group and say, "Let's all worry about it." He just shook it off back into the fire.

It reminds me of the story of an old farmer who had a mule, and the mule somehow fell into a well. He had no way of getting the mule out, and he didn't know what to do. So, he just thought he would put the mule out of its misery. He thought, *I'm just going to bury it.* So, he started shoveling dirt into the well.

Every time a shovel-load of dirt would hit that mule, it would shake it off and stamp on it. Shovel load after shovel load, he would shake off that dirt and then pack it down, until he eventually worked his way to the top and could get out of the well. That is a pretty good way to handle worry. When things happen, shake them off, and turn your worries into worship. Let them raise you up.

Wiz Khalifa said about worry, "Worry is like walking around with an umbrella, waiting for it to rain." Someone else said that he stopped being afraid of what could go *wrong* and started focusing on what could go *right.* Give faith an equal chance. Worrying is using your imagination to create things that you do not want.

Six Steps for Overcoming Worry

Let me give you six things you can to do to help you overcome worry. Number one is this:

Realize God Will Use it for Good

Realize that God will use it for good. Whatever you are going through, God is going to take it and use it for your good and for His glory. Remember what Romans 8:28 says.

Romans 8:28

All things work together for good to those that love God and that are called according to His purpose.

That just simply means that whatever you are facing, God is going to turn it around and cause it to benefit you and not harm you. Don't go past this too quickly. What God is saying is that it ain't over 'til it's over. That thing in your life, that problem that is giving you so much grief, pain, heartache, and has wounded you so deeply, God is saying, "I'm going to turn that thing around and turn that pain into a blessing."

If you are going through something, let me just go ahead and tell you, God is getting ready to bless you and take you to a whole new level. God specializes in bringing good out of bad.

Now, I did not say that God brings bad situations. But, He will take any bad situation you are in, turn it around, and bring good out of it, to benefit you and to glorify Him.

That promise in Romans 8:28 is not for everyone; it is specifically for those who commit to following Him. You might say, "Pastor, my situation is too bad. It is too far gone. It is too difficult. Nothing good can come from this." Let me just remind you that God took a cross, a tool of execution, and He turned it around to bless you, me, and countless other people.

God can take the worst, most impossible situation and turn it around for His glory. I challenge you today to trust God.

Refuse to Fear

The second principle to follow, is that you have to refuse to fear. You have got to refuse to be afraid. Whenever you hit a wall or face a storm, one thing that happens is that Satan's propaganda machine goes into full force. 24/7 he is cranking out all of these terrible things that can happen.

You have all of these scenarios running through your mind of how bad it is going to be or how impossible it is going to get, and Satan works overtime trying to create within you the spirit of fear.

But God says, "I have not given you the spirit of fear." Take that sound mind that has been renewed by the Word of God and that love that God has for you to remove all fears. You have got to refuse to be afraid. Let me share just a couple of verses from Psalm 91. This is a great psalm that you ought to have earmarked in your Bible.

Psalm 91:1-6

He who dwells in the shelter of the Most High will abide in the shadow of the Almighty. I will say to the Lord, "My refuge and my fortress, my God, in whom I trust." For he will deliver you from the snare of the fowler and from the deadly pestilence. He will cover you with his pinions, and under his wings you will find refuge; his faithfulness is a shield and buckler. You will not fear the terror of the night, nor the arrow that flies by day, nor the pestilence that stalks in darkness, nor the destruction that wastes at noonday.

This is a psalm of protection. Psalms 91 is what I call *God's 911*. The first thing he says is that when you face fear or worry, run to God, and spend that time in His presence. It goes on to say that when you are in an impossible situation, when you should be afraid, the best thing you can do is worship God and trust Him in that situation. God's got your back. He is going to get you through that storm you are facing.

Rejoice in Your Circumstance

The third principle that I want to give you is, rejoice in your circumstance. Philippians chapter four says:

Philippians 4:4

Rejoice in the Lord always and again, I say, Rejoice.

This verse is not telling you to rejoice because of your problems. What it is saying is that your rejoicing should be in the Lord, rather than focusing on or worrying about your problem. Rejoice that whatever you are going through, God is going to turn it around. You might be facing a storm, but God is going to turn it into a blessing.

Recruit People

The fourth thing that I want to tell you about facing the storm is, you have to recruit. People are so valuable in your life when you are going through something, and you need to find the right people to surround you. I like to say it this way: People are like elevators. They are either going to take you up to a higher level, or they are going to take you down to a floor you don't want to go to. You need to be careful when you are facing a storm who you surround yourself with, because there are a lot of negative people who will feed your fears and cause you to go down to that lower level.

Surround yourself with people who have big faith. Surround yourself with people who are positive, big-hearted, and generous. Surround yourself with people who are faith-filled, Spirit-filled, and love God. They will help you to weather the storm you are facing. It is so important.

I promise you, when you get two or three negative people together, you are not going to get an optimists' club. There is no way you are going to get a good forecast about what you are going through. So, recruit people. Find those people you can draw close to you who are going to lift you and take you to another level.

Live One Day at a Time

Number five for overcoming worry is this: When you are facing a storm or going through a trial, live your life one day at a time. Jesus taught that principle. If you are lifting a bar that has the amount of weight on it that is typically what you work out with, you are comfortable with that; you can do that. But each time you put another plate on that bar, it begins to get heavier and take away your energy.

If you do what you are comfortable with, you can lift that weight, but when you begin to borrow the weight from tomorrow, when you begin to take everybody else's weights and put them on that bar, it is not going to be long before you will be crushed under the weight of everybody else's problems and worries. Just do what you can do. Don't borrow worry from friends. Don't borrow worry from tomorrow. Don't worry about the past. Trust God with those things that are in your life right now.

Make the Choice to Rejoice

The last thing that I would say about worry is to make the choice to rejoice. When you wake up every morning, you have the choice to be happy or unhappy. You get to choose how you are going to face the day. You can choose to say, "I am going to have a good day," or "I am going to have a bad day."

Remember when David made the statement, "This is the day the Lord has made. I will rejoice (Psalm 118:24)." Those words, I *will* mean "I *choose* to operate this way." David said. "I choose to have a good day. This is the day the Lord has made. I will rejoice and be glad in it."

David did not say, "Tomorrow, I think I'll be happy." David didn't say, "Next week when I don't have so many worries, when I don't have so many problems, when I've ironed out all the wrinkles of my life, then I'll be happy."

Guess what? Life will pass you by, and you will have missed it. Happiness is a decision you make and not an emotion you feel. Psalms 150:6 is great advice. It says:

Psalm 150:6

Let everything that has breath praise the Lord.

Now, I know when you feel like the world is crushing you and pressing in on you, you do not feel like praising God. That's all right, because it did not say you had to feel like it; it just said, if you have breath, go ahead and praise God for whatever situation you are in.

I mentioned David just a moment ago. If you read about the life of David, throughout the Bible, you find out that David was without a doubt, one of the greatest worshippers in the Bible. He wrote so many of the Psalms, and he lived a life of worship. God said about David, "He is a man after my own heart."

David learned how to praise God in good times and in bad times. When you begin to read his life and recount the things that he went through, David, in the middle of battle, praised God. David, when he was surrounded by the enemy, cut off from family, cut off from home, cut off from everything, praised God. David, when he was living in a cave, running for his life, praised God. He lived a lifestyle of praise even in the midst of the many troubles that he had to face.

Some people look at life, and they see it as just problem after problem after problem. They think, *All I have to do is solve the next problem. As soon as I solve all of these problems, I can be happy.* You can be happy before any problem is ever solved, because it is a choice you make.

Proverbs 12:25 says, "An anxious heart weighs a man down." It creates heaviness in your life. Philippians 4:6 says, "Be anxious for nothing, but in everything, give thanks. And Paul says to turn every worry into worship. If you have something you are worrying about today, just begin to praise God for a favorable outcome in your life.

Do you remember the toy, Stretch Armstrong? You would grab him, and one of the fun things to do was to stretch it as far as you could, let go, and smack your brother in the face. That always started a good fight around my house.

Some of you feel under such stress and such worry that you feel like that Stretch Armstrong toy. How much further can you go? How much more can you bear?

Let me tell you this: The Bible very clearly says that God will not put more on you or will not allow more to be put on you than what you can handle (1 Corinthians 10:13). You are stronger than you think you are, and right now, you may feel like you are stretched to a breaking point. But God knows exactly where you are, what you are facing, and what you are going through. He is strengthening you right now.

When I was a kid, my dad prided himself on how far he could go on a tank of gas. Some of you are the same way. He would purposely drive past gas stations to go into the next town, saying, "I've got this. We can make it." He had no greater joy in life than when the car was coughing, spattering, and about to die, to just cruise in on the last vapor of gas into the service station to the pump. That was a major victory for him.

There are a lot of people who live life that way. "If I can just make it through..." Worry robs you of your joy. Worry robs you of your spiritual strength. Worry robs you of all the things that God wants to do in you. I am telling you, stop the worry, and start to praise. You are stronger than you think you are. God will get you through the storm you are facing.

There was a song that we used to teach in Sunday school called, "He's Got the Whole World in His Hands". I love the picture that paints. First of all, it says that we have this huge, giant, enormous God that the Bible says has the whole world in the palms of His hands. We serve a big, big God who does big, big things, and this God has big plans for your life.

This huge, enormous God that we are talking about knows who you are, where you are, and what you are facing. He has a purpose. Psalms 8:4 says:

Psalms 8:4

What is man that you are mindful of him and you have visited him?

The number one reason we struggle with worry is because we believe we are too common. There are seven billion people on planet Earth. We think, *How could this huge God even know who I am or where I am?* And we get this feeling that we are an insignificant speck. But the Bible says that God knows who you are and where you are. He has numbered the very hairs of your head (Luke 12:7). He knows your thoughts before you think them.

Jeremiah writes that God says, "I know the plans I have for you, plans to give you a future and a hope (Jeremiah 29:11)." We struggle sometimes, because we think, *Who am I that God even knows me?* I am telling you, God knows everything about you. In fact, in Luke's Gospel, the 15th chapter, Jesus was trying to communicate to the people around Him just how much God loves them.

When you think somebody does not care, or if you think God is not interested, it creates worry. But in Luke 15, Jesus used three parables (stories) to show people how much God loves them. The first example that He gave was of a widow woman who was looking for a lost coin. She had a full jar of coins, but she lost one. However, she didn't say, "Oh well. It's no big deal. It's just a penny." The parable said that she turned that house over. She looked under everything, turned every piece of furniture over, and swept the entire house out until she found that one penny.

God was saying, "You are that penny." He will never stop looking for you, caring for you, and searching for you. And then Jesus gave another example about a shepherd who had 100 sheep. But when he took inventory that night, he realized one of the sheep was missing. Instead of saying, "Well, I'll just write that off as a business loss," or "You win some; you lose some," he put the 99 in care of someone else, and he risked everything to go out at night looking for that lost sheep. Jesus said, "You are that lost sheep. God will search for you and look for you because He cares that much about you."

The third example that He gave was the example of the prodigal son. Here was someone who had run away from the father, and even though he had run away, the father never stopped caring, never stopped loving, never stopped waiting for that child to return.

I want you to get a picture of how much God loves you, how concerned He is about what you are facing, the pressure that you are feeling, and what you are going through. You are not alone. If God is for you, who can be against you (Romans 8:31)? God wants you to go through that storm with Him holding you and creating that environment of peace and love to walk you through. So, whatever your worries are today, I want you to know God knows who you are. God knows what you are facing.

Review

Worry can be paralyzing. It can lead to health problems, and ultimately, it is telling God that we do not trust Him. God has proven Himself trustworthy, He has proven that He loves us, and He promises never to leave us. Worry is natural, but if we are in Christ, we have no reason to be afraid. Choose to reject fear, trust God, and rejoice.

In the next chapter, we will tackle depression, and sometimes worry can lead to depression. Many people in the Bible even had seasons of despair. We will look at their lives and some common causes of non-clinical depression, so you can learn how to overcome it.

Take Action

1. Pinpoint an area in which you frequently worry. Pray for God's help in that specific area.

_____

_____

2. Write out the reasons why you should not worry, and post them where you will see them often.

_____

_____

_____

CHAPTER SIX

DEPRESSION

L et's begin by reading from the book of Job to talk about weathering the storm of depression.

Job 3:1-10

After this, Job opened his mouth and cursed the day of his birth. And Job said:

"Let the day perish on which I was born, and the night

that said, 'A man is conceived.'

Let that day be darkness!

May God above not seek it, nor light shine upon it.

Let gloom and deep darkness claim it.

Let clouds dwell upon it; let the blackness of the day

terrify it.

That night—let thick darkness seize it!

Let it not rejoice among the days of the year; let it not

come into the number of the months.

Behold, let that night be barren; let no joyful cry enter it.

Let those curse it who curse the day, who are ready to

rouse up Leviathan.

Let the stars of its dawn be dark; let it hope for light, but

have none, nor see the eyelids of the morning,

because it did not shut the doors of my mother's

womb, nor hide trouble from my eyes.

Why did I not die from the womb?

Why did I not give up the ghost when my mother bore me?

That is a whole lot more than just having a bad day, right? This is a major episode of depression that Job is going through.

The number one emotional problem in America today is depression. 60% of Americans are on prescription drugs, with the majority being antidepressants or painkillers. Americans make up four to five percent of the world's population, and yet we use 80% of the world's medication.[5]

Something is wrong with that picture. We need help. When it comes to depression, whether you are feeling blue, having a Monday all week saying, "I'm not happy," or even if you sing the song "Gloom, Despair and Agony on Me", everyone battles with depression in their lives.

Now, I am not talking about clinical depression. I am talking about moods that we get in that we have to work through. There is a phrase in the Bible that is used to describe depression, and it is very fitting and accurate. That phrase is a "spirit of heaviness". Depression can very accurately be described as a heaviness, whether it is in your mind, in your emotions, or physically affecting your body.

People who have had depression have even described it as being like an elephant sitting on their chest or a huge weight pressing them down, holding them in place and stopping them from moving forward. But the Bible also uses the word *spirit*. It is a spirit of heaviness, meaning that often, depression is a spiritual matter or is a matter of spiritual warfare.

Often, depression can be linked to a spiritual attack. In fact, I am going to go a little further and say it this way: Depression is often a direct, demonic assignment against you for the purpose of discouraging you, deflating you, creating fear in your life, and driving a wedge between you and God.

Now, I am not saying that every time you are feeling blue or having a bad day, the enemy is camped out on your doorstep. I am telling you that there is a very real devil that the Bible says comes to steal, kill, and destroy (John 10:10).

He wants to kill your joy, your peace of mind, and your quality of life. The Bible says that Satan goes about as a roaring lion, seeking whom he may devour (1 Peter 5:8). Think about that for just a moment. He is seeking out a weak link. He is looking for an area of vulnerability in your life that he can camp out on, magnify, and begin to break down.

Isaiah 61:13 tells us that there is a spirit of heaviness that comes against us, and it also tells us what the cure is for a spirit of heaviness. The Bible says to put on the garment of praise for the spirit of heaviness. In fact, it literally says to be "wrapped in praise".

The picture that comes to mind when I think of somebody living a life that is wrapped in praise is a person wrapped in bubble wrap. Someone wrapped in bubble wrap would be pretty well prepared for anything that comes his or her way.

Spiritually, when we live a life wrapped in praise, we have a greater defense against the enemy. When we live a life wrapped in praise, we say, "I'm going to have a lifestyle of praise. I'm going to live a lifestyle of giving glory to God. I'm going to be quick to exalt Him. I want to be quick to turn my problems over to Him." When we live life like that, we are protected from the repeated attacks of the enemy.

Everyone faces depression at some point. You can even read through the Bible and find a long list of people who faced it. For example, Abraham, the original faith man, the father of our faith, dealt with depression.

Moses did, too. In fact, Moses lived a life of incredible highs, living on the mountaintop and then in the valley, as well. Elijah, the great prophet and miracle worker, suffered from depression. He even prayed the prayer, "God, take my life (1 Kings 19:4)." *That* is a depressed person!

David also faced depression. In Psalm 43, David wrote, "Why art thou cast down, oh my soul? Hope thou in God." To be *cast down* was a phrase that every shepherd understood, because it meant a sheep had fallen over on its side and ended up on its back. When that sheep was in that position, there was no way that he could right himself or get himself off of his back.

If a sheep is downcast, it also means that he is very vulnerable and open to attack from anything that comes his way. If he lays there too long, he is going to die, not just from the elements, not just from the attacks, but it creates poisonous gases in his stomach, which can cause him to die. So when a sheep is cast down, he is totally helpless.

Now remember, he is talking about a picture of us. When the shepherd shows up, he realizes he has got to restore the sheep. Psalm 23 is also a psalm about sheep. David said about our God that "He restores my soul." Let me tell you what the restoration process looked like.

He did not just immediately pick the sheep up, but there was a process. The first thing he did was massage the legs of the sheep and then turn it on its side. He then would massage the legs of the sheep again to create circulation. After that, he would stand it up and hold it there until its equilibrium came back. After a period of holding it there (this process took 30 to 40 minutes), he would release it back into the fold.

God is a God who restores. We all love it when God does the instant thing, the instant miracle, or the instant answer to prayer. But there are times when we go through a restoration *process*. There are times when God works us through our situation. It is a great time of learning and discipleship, and God has wisdom on how to bring us out of what we are going through. He is the good shepherd who restores us back to that place where we need to be.

What Jesus Did

As you read through the Bible, you find out that even Jesus had a battle with depression. In fact, let's look at it in Matthew chapter 26. We are going to look at Jesus' plan for how to handle depression.

Matthew 26:36-45

Then Jesus went with his disciples to a place called Geth-semane, and he said to them, "Sit here while I go over there and pray." He took Peter and the two sons of Zebedee along with him, and he began to be sorrowful and troubled. Then he said to them, "My soul is overwhelmed with sorrow to the point of death. Stay here and keep watch with me."

Going a little farther, he fell with his face to the ground and prayed, "My Father, if it is possible, may this cup be taken from me. Yet not as I will, but as you will."

Then he returned to his disciples and found them sleeping. "Couldn't you men keep watch with me for one hour?" he asked Peter. "Watch and pray so that you will not fall into temptation. The spirit is willing, but the flesh is weak."

He went away a second time and prayed, "My Father, if it is not possible for this cup to be taken away unless I drink it, may your will be done."

When he came back, he again found them sleeping, be-cause their eyes were heavy. So he left them and went away once more and prayed the third time, saying the same thing.

Then he returned to the disciples and said to them, "Are you still sleeping and resting? Look, the hour has come, and the Son of Man is delivered into the hands of sinners.

Look at what Jesus did when he was facing the most difficult time of his life.

He Prayed

Jesus went through this emotional time of struggling spiritually and physically. He said, "I am so overburdened. I am so overpowered by what is going on right now. I feel like I am going to die." But let's see what He did in order to turn this situation around. The first thing that jumps out is that He prayed. And He did not just *sort of* pray. He *really* prayed. This was not one of those "in and out" prayers, a light prayer, or a quick prayer. This was deep intercession.

There are some things in life that cannot be solved with a sixty-second prayer or a five-minute devotion. There are some things in life that are going to require a *season* of prayer. They are going to require you to spend significant time in prayer, a time of deep intercession, praying for your circumstance. It may be days. It may be weeks. It may be months.

He Surrounded Himself With People

The next thing that He did was surround Himself with people. He brought His disciples with Him. One of the things that Satan loves to do is to insulate and isolate us from other people when we go through hard times.

In fact, when you are battling depression and you are going through a difficult time, often one of the first things you say is, "Leave me alone. Don't bother me. Don't talk to me. I don't want to be bothered by anyone."

In that moment of weakness, Satan moves in and begins to exploit our thoughts and get us thinking in the wrong direction, and it takes us in the direction that we would not ordinarily go if we had people in our lives.

Now, let me just make a statement of something that I have seen happen over and over again in ministry. Loneliness makes people do stupid things. I am not saying people *are* stupid. I am just saying loneliness makes people *do* stupid things. Loneliness makes people make bad decisions that they would not ordinarily make, and when you are going through a difficult time, you do not need to isolate yourself. You need to bring people into your life who can help you think this thing through and figure it out.

Do you realize that loneliness was the very first thing to which God looked and said, "That's not good" (Genesis 2:18)? Remember, God created Adam, looked at him while he was all alone and said, "That's not a good thing that man is alone." It is one thing to have solitude; that is good and refreshing. But isolation is destructive. So find people in your life who can help you get through what you are going through.

Mother Teresa, who really understood poverty and lived with impoverished people, said, "Loneliness is the most terrible poverty." - to not have people around you who can lift you and encourage you. Ecclesiastes 4:10 says, "Woe unto him that is alone when he falls, for he has no one to pick him up." We need relationships in our lives. We need people who can lift us and encourage us. We need people who can be there for us. Find those people in your life, and draw them near.

He Did Not Stay There

The third thing that Jesus did is, He did not stay there. Jesus prayed and had that moment of saying to his disciples, "All right, go ahead and sleep, because in the morning, we are going to hit the ground running." He got up and got out of that place of discouragement.

If you are in a place of discouragement, let me just say first of all, try not to go there in the first place. There are certain places you should not let your thinking take you. There are certain places you just do not go emotionally, because nothing good is going to come out of it. Have you ever been driving and you took a wrong turn and headed down the wrong street? What did you do? Did you just keep going? Somewhere down the road, you have got to say, "Whoa, wait a minute. I need to turn this thing around and go in another direction."

The same is true emotionally. If you are going down somewhere and it is bringing discouragement and doubt, do not go there thought-wise. Do not focus on that. Turn around, and head in a different direction.

A number of years ago, as I was going to visit my pastor who lived in Fort Worth, I was driving late at night, and I thought, *I am going to get something to keep me awake, a snack and a Coke or something.* I saw a convenience store that was a good distance off the highway, but I could see it. I thought, *I'll just exit here and get a Coke and a bag of chips to keep going.* I turned down that road, and halfway down that road, I saw a car that was pulled over with two men standing beside it.

I am not normally prone to fear. In fact, usually I would stop and say, "Hey, can I help you guys?" But there was something on the inside that said, "Turn around. Don't even go there. Don't go against your better judgment." I've learned through the years to listen to that inward voice.

So, I just simply turned the car around, got back on the highway, and started going in another direction.

I do not know what might have happened, if anything, but thank God I know how to hear the voice of the Holy Spirit! And there are times when the Holy Spirit will tell you, "Don't go there. Turn around. Nothing good is going to come out of that. Get back going in the right direction." Listen to Him when He tells you that.

Four Causes of Depression

I would like to give you four causes of depression. There are more than four, obviously, but these are four that I think are very standard.

Disappointment

Number one is disappointment. Disappointment comes in all shapes and sizes. It could be because you got told, "No," or you did not get something you wanted. Disappointments can come through breaking up in a relationship or a divorce. That is a little bit further up the food chain, but that can bring discouragement and disappointment.

The top of the list is probably the loss of a child, a miscarriage, or the loss of a loved one. That also triggers disappointment.

But the point is, we all face disappointments. They may be small, or they may be big. But, we all face them, and one of the most common causes of disappointment is unrealistic expectations. -not in God, because God never disappoints, but disappointment in people.

Can I just tell you something about people? People will let you down. People will fail you. It is because people are a lot like you. They are imperfect. They have problems. They are very human, just like you are. Put your faith and trust in God, not people.

Here is an action step that you can take: If you are facing a disappointment, I want you to own it. What I mean is, I want you to embrace that disappointment. I want you to say, "Yeah, this happened in my life. It is what it is. I understand. I wish my life were different, but I am battling disappointment." I want you to own it. I want you to learn from it. I want you to grow from it. Then, I want you to turn around and help someone else get through what they are going through.

Let me give you a great example. Do you remember the story of Bethany Hamilton? She was a young star at 13 or 14 years old who was surfing, when a 1,500 pound shark attacked her and bit her arm off. Now listen to what she said right after this happened. She said, "I'm going to go with it. God's got this."

A shark biting off your arm can definitely trigger disappointments. But she said, "I'm going to go with this. God's got this," and just three months later, she was back in the water, surfing competitively. And a lot of that had to do with her attitude of embracing what had happened in her life. "This has happened, but I'm going to go forward. My life is still in front of me."

Low Self-Esteem

The second cause of depression is low self-esteem. One of the things the Bible says is that we are to love our neighbors as we love ourselves. That is fundamental to Christianity. In fact, if you do not love yourself, you cannot love your neighbor. If you do not like yourself, it is pretty much a given that you are not going to like other people, which makes it impossible for you to fulfill God's commandment to love your neighbor as yourself.

I want you to remember this: You are valuable even if you do not feel like it. Do you know why? -because God determines your value, not people. God determines your value, not circumstances. God determines your value and not the emotions you are feeling. Let me back that up with Scripture. Psalms 139:14 says:

Psalms 139:14

I praise you because I am fearfully and wonderfully made. Wonderful are your works, and I know that full well.

There is another version of that same verse that says, "Thank you for making me so wonderfully complex. Your workmanship is marvelous." Get this into your thinking. Let it become a part of the core of who you are. A poor self-image is an insult to the God who made you. Think about that for just a moment.

A poor self-image is an insult to the God who made you.

If you have a poor self-image, that tells me two things right off the bat. Number one, it tells me that you do not read your Bible. Number two, it tells me you do not believe the Bible when you do read it. Ouch...

There is no way you can read and believe the Bible and not like yourself, because of what God says about you. Over and over again, the Bible says great things about who you are. The Bible is a book that repeatedly tells you you are somebody, that you have value, that you matter, and you are the very apple of His eye.

When I was in Bible school, one of my instructors encouraged our class to do an exercise. It was to go through certain epistles (Galatians, Ephesians, Philippians, Colossians...) and just read those letters to the church, as if God wrote those for them.

And everywhere that it says *you* or *me* or *we*, I told people to put their name in there and realize what God says about them spiritually, how God thinks about them, and the rights and privileges that God has given. If you begin to do that, I promise you, it will change your life and the way you think about yourself and others.

Unrealistic Expectations

The third major cause of depression is unrealistic expectations. Do not make the mistake of comparing yourself to others. Let me tell you why that is a bad idea. There is always going to be someone better than you. There is always going to be someone who is a better athlete, has a better job, a prettier spouse, smarter kids, more money, gets all the breaks, a nicer car... There is always going to be someone better than you.

When you begin to compare yourself with others, that is a lose-lose situation. Stop. All you are doing is depressing yourself. You just need to realize that God has given you a specific assignment. Let God make you what He wants you to be.

During the Academy Awards season in Hollywood, all of the stars and celebrities show up. They walk this thing called the red carpet, and one of the questions they are always asked (especially the ladies) is, "Who are you wearing?" -meaning, "Who designed your dress?" It is a class thing or a prestige and value thing.

Can I just remind you of something, Child of God? You are a designer original. God created you. God made you. You are wearing God, and you could not look better. Just understand that you are someone, and God is your designer. Get comfortable in your own skin. Learn to be content and happy with who you are. Learn to be happy with where you are, and then when you understand that, let God make you everything that He wants you to be. In other words, quit questioning God, and start trusting Him.

I love the story from the Bible about a guy named Mephibosheth. Not a lot of said about him, but what is said is powerful. Mephibosheth was the son of Jonathan, David's best friend, and Mephibosheth was King Saul's grandson. When Saul and Jonathan were killed in battle, there was a messenger who came to Jonathan's house and said, "You guys have got to get out of here because the Philistines are coming, and they are going to totally wipe out Saul's lineage."

So, the head maid and nurse grabbed up this baby, this young man. She began running with him and dropped him, breaking both of his ankles. So, for the rest of his life, he lived crippled.

A number of years go by, David gets back, and he establishes his kingdom. After a while, he is feeling a little melancholy. One day, he begins to ask himself and ask around, "Is there anyone from my friend Jonathan's family that I can bless? Does anybody remain from his family?"

And one person remembered that Jonathan had a son by the name of Mephibosheth. David said, "Go find him, and bring him to me." When they found Mephibosheth, he was broken. He was living a life of poverty, and he was fearful. In fact, when they said, "King David wants to see you," Mephibosheth said, "I'm a dead dog. He's going to bring me to the castle to kill me."

We do that with God sometimes. We are afraid to go to the one who wants to bless and heal us. Maybe we made a mistake, and we are running *from* God rather than *to* Him.

They brought Mephibosheth to David, and David said, "Son, everything that I have is yours. You always have a seat at my table." Man, I love that story, because that is what God does with every one of us who will let Him! He restores us. He gives us a seat at the table and puts us in a relationship. You are the apple of His eye. You are loved by God.

Holding on to Guilt

The fourth cause of depression is holding on to guilt. Nothing creates depression faster than living under guilt and condemnation. And yet, so many people live their lives that way. Psalms 38 says:

Psalm 38:4-6

My guilt has overwhelmed me like a burden too heavy to bear... I am bowed down and brought low; all day long I go about mourning.

Does that sound like depression? That is exactly what that is. That is depression described. So what do we do with guilt? We face it. All of us have fallen short of the glory of God (Romans 3:23). You could cover up your guilt, but you know that does not work, right? I describe it this way: Covering up guilt is like hiding a body in the trunk of your car (not that I know anything about that).

It never goes away. You are constantly aware of it. You constantly feel this need that says, "I've got to deal with it. I've got to fix it. I've got to hide it more." You cannot cover it up; it does not work. So that is not the approach that you want to take.

The next thing that people try to do when guilt comes is, they try to rationalize it. In other words, they try to reason in their minds, *It's not hurting anyone. It's no big deal. Everyone's doing it.* You know what the word rationalize means? It means to tell yourself rational lies.

You lie to yourself, hide the truth, skirt the real issue, and make yourself feel good. You convince yourself that what you are telling yourself is the right thing when you know it is not. So, that does not work.

The next thing that people do when they try to deal with guilt is, they punish themselves. Have you ever been there? "If I just beat myself up long enough, maybe somewhere down the road, I'll feel better."

I have an illustration from my grandkids about beating yourself up. All three of my grandkids one day were up in my daughter's room, playing around. And the big brother, Landon, usually plays one of two roles. He is either guardian of the galaxy, watching over his sisters, or he is the constant thorn in their flesh. And sometimes it turns on a dime.

One particular day, he was the guardian of the universe, and the little one, Charlie, picks up something and throws it at her sister. Landon runs over right away, being the big brother, the teacher, and the protector, looks at Charlie and he kneels down saying, "No no, Charlie!" and he pats her on the face. He did not hurt her, but he broke her heart. She just started crying big crocodile tears; it was a bad scene.

So my daughter, Evelyn, picked her up, carried Charlie downstairs, handed her to her mom, and said, "Here's what happened: Landon wasn't being mean. She just got her feelings hurt. It's all good." And so, Evelyn turns to go back upstairs to her room.

When she gets up the stairs, she finds out the door to her room is closed, and Kinley, the other sister, is sitting on the steps. As Evelyn gets up to her, Kinley stands up, holds up her hand, and says, "I have to warn you; Landon is hiding because he's ashamed."

She opens the door, and she can hear Landon crying, but she cannot find him. He has shoved himself under the bed and is crying his eyes out because he felt like he hurt his sister.

Eventually he got over it, but isn't that what we do? We run from God, and we hide. We carry all this guilt ourselves rather than giving it to God. Evelyn told him, "Nobody's mad at you. It's all right. You don't have to do this. You're not in trouble."

Let me just tell you, you do not have to run from God. You do not have to carry the guilt. Roman 3:23 says, "All have sinned and fallen short of the glory of God."

The Bible says all of us have sinned. God said, "I've got this. I've taken care of that. Everything that you have done, every sin that you're doing now, every sin that you're going to do, I forgive it. You just need to bring it to me and let me take away the guilt. Let me take away the shame, and let us be in a right relationship."

The most basic truth of Christianity is that Jesus Christ died to forgive all of your sins. He has already done that.

Let me share this last Scripture with you. It is from Matthew chapter five, and this one is from *The Message* Bible:

Matthew 5:3

You are blessed when you're at the end of your rope. With less of you, there is more of God.

If you feel like you are at the end of your rope, you do not know what to do, and you do not know how much longer you can hold on, let me just say what the Bible says. You are in a blessed place, because God is getting ready to show up in your life. In your weakness, He reveals His strength. At your lowest point, God's power becomes greatest in your life. I am not minimizing what you are going through, and I am not saying it is not a big deal. But *God* is saying it is not a big deal. I cannot say that, But God can.

Review

Depression is extremely common in our society. When life gets hard, as it eventually does for everyone, it can be difficult *not* to become depressed and hopeless. Even many of our heroes from the Bible had bouts of depression. However, there is a way out. Our hope, confidence, and joy comes from the Lord. With time, prayer, and truth from the Bible, He can lead you to victory.

Our next and final chapter is about rebuilding after a storm. Maybe you are coming out of a time of worry and depression, and you are ready to move forward. Maybe you are still in the thick of a storm, but you want to look ahead and start preparing for an eventual end and rebuilding time. The next chapter will primarily use the book of Nehemiah as a blueprint on how to move into a brighter future.

Take Action

1. What is a common cause of depression for you? List out people you can talk to when those times come.

_____

_____

_____

2. If you are currently depressed, contact your church or a friend to pray with you. Or, reach out to a local counseling center to talk through what might be keeping you stuck.

CHAPTER SEVEN

REBUILDING AFTER A STORM

This may be the most important chapter in this book, because we are talking about rebuilding after a storm and moving past it into the future. If you have just come out of a storm or are almost through one, this is really going to speak to what to do and where to go from here.

I want to start off with a couple of foundational, basic Bible Scriptures, and both are from the book of Isaiah.

Isaiah 43:19

Behold, I will do a new thing. Now it shall spring forth. I will even make a way in the wilderness and rivers in the desert.

That is a great word from God's heart to your heart. And then the other verse for encouragement is Isaiah chapter 42:9. God again is speaking, and He says:

Isaiah 42:9

Behold, the former things have come to pass and new things do I declare. I'm speaking new things over your life, and before they spring forth, I will tell you of them.

God might already be starting a new season or a new day in your life. If you want God to do a new thing (and I know that sounds like insanity, because who wouldn't want God to do a new thing in their life?), He is going to require a couple of things from you. Number one, He is going to require *more* of you.

There are a lot of people who are comfortable in their worn-out dreams and in their old way of doing things, and they are comfortable right where they are. They would kind of like things to be better, but not if they have to raise the bar on themselves.

What God Asks of You

If God is going to do a new thing, here is the idea: What got you *here* will not get you *there*. God is asking you to bring your "A game". He is going to ask you to dig in and believe Him.

The second thing that God is going to ask from you is greater faith. Now, why is that? Often, we get comfortable in our circumstances. I like what one man said when he put it this way: "Circumstances are like a mattress. If you get on top of them, you can rest comfortably. But if you get underneath them, they'll suffocate you." Often, that is how we feel about our problems. Faith begins to look beyond circumstances. 2 Corinthians 4:18 says that we fix our eyes not on what is seen.

God is saying, "Don't focus on what you see. Focus on what you *don't* see." Let me explain what that means. What is seen is the problem, which is temporary. But what is unseen is God's power, which is eternal.

So, here is the good news: Your problem is temporary. I did not say it wasn't big or intimidating. I just said it is temporary. It is not going to be around forever...but God will be.

There is an expiration date on your problem, but God never changes. God, who we cannot see with our eye, has power that is eternal. If you can see it, you can change it by the power of faith. Everything is subject to change by faith, as we talked about earlier in this book.

Faith is not denying your reality. Faith is not denying the circumstances or saying, "I'm not in pain," when I am. Faith is not saying that you do not hurt when you really do, that you are not grieving when you are, or that you are happy when really, on the inside, you are broken up. That is not faith. That is phony.

God is not into phony or fake. What is faith? Faith is simply facing reality without being discouraged by it. So, do not deny that you have problems. Rather, know that you can face your problems because God is more real than the reality you are looking at.

Here is the good news: You can build or rebuild your marriage today by faith. You can build or rebuild your business by faith. You can build or rebuild your life if you simply have faith in God.

How to Rebuild

Let's look at Nehemiah chapter two. We are going to look at what it takes to rebuild after a storm. Now, remember that Nehemiah was the guy who was responsible for rebuilding the walls of Jerusalem. He had been taken captive. The walls of Jerusalem had been destroyed, and Nehemiah gets word of it. God ultimately uses him to rebuild the walls. In chapter two, verse two, he gets the news that things are bad back home, and he is an assistant to the king. He says:

Nehemiah 2:

Therefore, the king said to me, Why is your face sad since you're not sick? This is nothing but sorrow of heart. So I became dreadfully afraid, and I said to the king, "May the king live forever. Why should my face not be said when the city, the place of my fathers lies waste and its gates are burned with fire?" Then the king said, "Well, what do you want?" So I prayed to the God of Heaven, and I said to the king, "If it pleases the king, if your servant has found favor in your sight, I ask that you send me to Jerusalem to the city of my father's tombs, that I may rebuild it."

The rest of this chapter and the other following chapters talk about what it took to rebuild the walls of Jerusalem once the king let him go, and I want to talk to you about what it takes to rebuild after a storm.

Vision

Number one: to rebuild takes vision. Nehemiah said, "I said to the king, 'If I have found favor in your sight that you would send me to Jerusalem, the city of my fathers, that I may rebuild it.'"

He had this mental picture of seeing the walls rebuilt and restored, and of worship returning to Jerusalem. If a city did not have walls, it could not protect the citizens. And nobody was going to move back to that city if they couldn't live behind a safe wall to be protected from enemies. Nehemiah knew that without that wall, the people could never worship God or restore their lives.

So he had this mental picture of people worshipping and seeing the glory of God return in their lives. And if you have ever walked through a storm, you need to begin to see yourself back in that right relationship with God, with God walking you through. And you need to draw close to God after the storm. Nehemiah had this vision of restoration.

Proverbs 29 says that where there is no vision, where there is no direction, the people perish. I like to turn that verse around and say that where there *is* a vision, the people flourish. If God is showing you something and speaking to you, He is taking you into a new season. But you have got to have a vision. You have got to *want* to fix your life. You have got to *want* to have a better future.

Remember I said earlier that your life does not automatically get better. You do not just get the life that you want; you *build* the life that you want. And maybe in this instance you RE-build the life that you want.

If you have just come through a storm, I want you to begin to think about what the future looks like. Get a mental picture of your life being restored, because when you have a vision of what you want your life to look like, God is going to add to that. You have to have a vision of getting it all back and then some.

I like those two words, *then some.* -because that is what God does. When God restores, He adds to it. Let me give you some examples. If you look at the book of Job, he lost everything. I mean, he lost it *all*. But at the end of the book, we found out that Job got everything back... and then some. Not only did he get everything back, what the Bible said is that God doubled it in his life.

Look at Joseph. Joseph was thrown into a pit by his brothers. He lost his position and his authority, but he got it all back. We think of the story of Joseph and his coat of many colors. It was not just a coat of many colors. Joseph did not walk out in this brand new jacket that had all of these wild colors in it, and his brothers were fashionistas, saying, "Man! We don't have a jacket like that." So, they threw him into a pit.

No, it was a coat that represented authority. This is why they got so mad. They did not get mad because he had some cool new clothes; they got mad because his father had given him a coat of authority, the family coat of arms, so to speak. When he walked out, they looked at him and basically, by the very clothes he wore, he was saying, "I have authority over you. I'm the chosen son. You will bow down to me now."

This was a dysfunctional family. They threw him in the pit, sold him into slavery, and got rid of him. But, Joseph got it all back... and then some. He got all of his authority back and ended up becoming number two in all of Egypt. He was the right hand man to Pharaoh.

Moses also lost it all and got it all back...and then some. The Bible said he gave up the riches of Pharaoh so that he could embrace God's greater riches.

Then you can even look at Jesus. Jesus lost it all. Jesus gave His life, but He got it back... and then some. You and I are the "then some" that Jesus got back. So, every time that you lose something, when God gives it back, he adds to it. And that is a Bible principle that we need to understand. He brings increase, and he adds to things.

This thing called vision gives us the heart to keep fighting. Vision gives us the heart to stay in there and keep doing what we are doing. Vision gives you the heart of a champion or an overcomer.

I love the story of a small businessman who had a small general store. A mega company came in and said, "We want to buy you out and build a whole new department store right here." He refused to sell and said, "This is my life. It's where I was grew up; my dad owned this store. I'm not selling." And they said, "Then we will drive you out of business."

So they bought everything around him and began to build their huge department store. They sandwiched him in, and finally, when all the construction dust had settled, they put two huge banners over the front of the building that said "Grand Opening". It just dwarfed his little store. But he had a plan of his own. He bought a banner and put it over the front of his store that said, "Main Entrance".

Let's hear it for the little guy! I love the attitude of an overcomer, and I love the heart of somebody who wants to finish. We serve a God who wants to do big things in our lives. But He wants us to think big thoughts. Take the limits off of your thinking. Start thinking God-sized thoughts. Dream big dreams, and pray big prayers.

Examination

The second thing it takes to rebuild is examination. In verse 13 of Nehemiah 2, it says that he went out by night. He went by the gate of the valley, and he viewed the walls of Jerusalem, which were broken down. The gates had been burned with fire.

Nehemiah went out at night and walked around the walls of the city. He found every broken down place that needed to be repaired, and this is the importance of examination: Before you are ready to rebuild, you really need to understand what got you there.

Now, I know that some storms just come for no reason other than to discourage us, but we have also talked about man-made storms, things that we do that put us in a position that opens us to the enemy, and we let down our guard. You need to look at your life, examine it, and ask, *Are there any broken down areas in my life that I need to rebuild?*

This whole thing about self-examination is to seek God. If I am the problem, I want God to show me where I went wrong or what I need to do. Look for those areas where you can close the door to the devil. Examine your life.

You have heard the phrase, "Check yourself before you wreck yourself." That is what I'm talking about. When you begin to examine the broken-down places of your life, maybe you can look at your passion and say, "I don't really know where my passion for God has gone."

The moment your passion for God begins to fade, you know that wall is broken down. *Why am I not as passionate about the things of God as I used to be? Why am I not on fire for God as I used to be? What did I let in that became a wedge between me and God or made me step back from God?*

Find out what that thing is, and examine it.

If you do not have the passion you once had, examine the wall. If there is trouble in your marriage or in other relationships, examine it. Ask, *What brought that problem into my marriage?* -because at one time, you and your spouse felt like you HAD to get married. You HAD to do life together. What happened to get you to the point that you can't stand each other? You have got to go back and ask, *Where did the problem start?*

Examine your priorities, your work, your time, and the words that come out of your mouth... Examine every area of your life. Sometimes the very words of our mouths tell us the content of our hearts. Listen to what you are saying about your life, your church, your work, or about your marriage, and then begin working right there. Change what you say.

Prayer

The third step to rebuilding is prayer. You cannot rebuild without prayer. Nehemiah 1:4 says:

Nehemiah 1:4

And it came to pass when I heard these words that the walls of Jerusalem were broken down. He said, "I sat down, I wept. I mourned, I fasted and I prayed before the God of Heaven."

You will never rebuild without prayer. If you try to build on any foundation other than the foundation of God's Word and a relationship with God, you are building on shifting sand. You have to begin to pray. Prayer is the conduit of Heaven and how you get Heaven on Earth.

Let me ask you a question. If you could ask God for any miracle and you knew that He would do it, what would you ask Him for? A better marriage? A better job? Healing for your body?

Jesus said, "Whatever you ask in my name, I will do it (John 14:14)." In fact, think about this. 1 John 5:14 says:

1 John 5:14

And this is the confidence that we have in him [him being Jesus, him being God] that if we ask anything according to his will, he hears us, and we know that we have the petition or the prayer answered that we desire of him.

That just simply says in black and white that God is a prayer-answering God, and you never rebuild your life until you begin to pray big prayers and invite God in. There is a saying that we have in our terminology, in our vernacular, that says, "Go big or go home." Basically, what that means is, when you show up, show up to be totally committed and involved. In your prayer life, start praying big prayers.

My friend, Wayne Myers, says it in a very interesting way. He says, "Aim for the stars, and you'll hit the moon. Aim for the ground, and you'll hit it every time." You need to pray big prayers in your life.

So, do not pray for a better marriage; pray for an *awesome* marriage. Do not pray that you get to feeling a little bit better; pray that you will have so much energy at the end of the day, you won't know what to do with yourself. Don't just pray to get a little closer to God and have a better relationship; pray to be filled with the Spirit and in a life-changing relationship with God.

In 1 Chronicles 4, there is the Prayer of Jabez. Now, the Bible does not give a lot of history about Jabez, but you can find a little about him, and this is one of the prayers that I pray. I have several things that I do each morning when I get up. It's not a ritual; it's a routine.

Some mornings I get up, and I just pray the Lord's Prayer, and it really directs my life. Other mornings I get up and pray the 23rd Psalm. I don't repeat it. I *pray* it. Sometimes I get up and just read a chapter, praying a chapter of the Bible.

And some mornings, when I get up, I go to the Prayer of Jabez in 1 Chronicles. I pray it over my life. Listen to what it says:

1 Chronicles 4:10

Jabez cried out to the God of Israel. "Oh, that you would bless me now and enlarge my territory indeed! Let your hand be with me. Keep me from harm so that I will be free from pain." And God granted his request.

God is a prayer-answering God. This is not a prayer of self-ishness. We are blessed in order to be a blessing, and Jabez is saying, "God, bless me; enlarge my territory." Territory means influence. "Let me have greater influence for the Kingdom of God. But God, bless my life so that I can be a blessing to someone else." God wants to bless you. Do not ever hesitate to ask God for a personal blessing.

There is a big prayer in Joshua chapter 10. As a little bit of history behind the story: Joshua was fighting five different armies, and these armies had plagued Israel from the very beginning. This battle is going on, and Joshua and Israel are winning against all of these enemies.

Then, Joshua has this revelation. He realizes that the sun is going down, and he is not going to have enough time to defeat the enemies. He has all this momentum, and he really wants to just wipe them out and be done with them once and for all.

He realizes, "I'm not going to be able to have enough daylight to fight this battle and win." So listen to what he prays: "God I'm asking you to make the sun stand still (Joshua 10)." Now, that is a God-size prayer! And the Bible says that God answered his prayer and extended the daylight so that Joshua could fight the battle.

Do not ever pray a small prayer with a God as big as ours. And when we say, "Sun, stand still," that is a metaphor for whatever your impossible situation is. It may be impossible to you, but it is not impossible to God. Pray that God-sized prayer. Pray what I call that "big, harry, audacious prayer" (like big, harry, audacious goals from Jim Collins). Pray those be BHAPs over your life.

Plan

Next, you've got to have a plan for your life. When you have a desire and you want to rebuild, that's great motivation.

I love this story about motivation. A guy is walking home one night, and he decides to take a shortcut through the cemetery. It is dark, but he could cut some minutes off of his walk home, and he walks right into a freshly open grave. It is dark, and he is in the middle of the cemetery all by himself. So, he starts trying to jump out of this grave.

He jumps and jumps for about 30 minutes, but he cannot get out of this grave. Finally, he accepts, *This is useless. I just have to wait here until the morning when people show up and get me out of here.* So he just consoles himself and realizes, *This is my situation,* and he just sits down at the end of the grave. A few minutes later, another guy takes a shortcut through the cemetery, and he falls into the open grave, too!

He is jumping and jumping, and finally, the guy sitting in the dark says to the other guy, "You can't get out of here." But immediately, he does! Sometimes all you need is that little extra bit of motivation.

You see, when we have a desire for something, and we really, really want it, we will develop a plan to get it. We will find a way. Where there's a will, there's a way. Where there is a desire, there is a pursuit, and you will find a way to get out of that situation and get what you want. If you will begin to pray, God will give you a plan and show you the steps to take to get out of your situation.

Make a plan, and if you are going to make a plan, part of it needs to be waiting on God. Sometimes we jump the gun way too early and get ahead of God. We need to learn to wait on Him. The book of Isaiah says:

Isaiah 40:31

Those that wait upon the Lord shall renew their strength. They shall mount up with wings as eagles. They'll run and not grow weary. They will walk and not faint.

There is something about when we stop and let God open the doors before us. One of the greatest lessons I have learned is that sometimes answered prayers have to unfold gradually. You have got to pray for patience. Are you impatient? Do you scream at the microwave? Do you get the shakes making instant coffee?

Some of us are impatient, but patience demonstrates faith in God. Patience says, "I know that God is working, and therefore, I don't have to be anxious, nervous, or upset, because I know God has got this. I am going to walk by faith." Part of your plan is that you need to live one day at a time.

Any man can fight a battle for a day, but when you begin to take tomorrow's problems and bring them into today and take yesterday's problems and bring them into today, you begin to get overwhelmed. Jesus said, "Just get through the day. There is enough stuff today to worry about (Matthew 6:34)". Just deal with what is on your plate today, and God will strengthen you and equip you for those challenges.

Part of your plan should also be to have right relationships. Get hooked up with people in your life who are going places. Understand the power of relationships. Some of you need new ones in your life, new people who have a vision, a goal, and a direction. It really is important. Who we hang out with changes the direction of our lives.

Your plan should also include new words. The words that come out of your mouth are either working *for* you or *against* you. I think about it this way: How different would your life be today if you were speaking more hope-filled, positive, and faith-filled words? Proverbs 18:21 says, "The power of life and death are in the tongue."

And then finally, you need to plan on sowing a seed. I don't think there is any other principle in the entire Word of God that is more life-changing or more powerful than the principle of seed time and harvest. Every one of us is sowing seeds for our tomorrow. Every word that we say, every action that we take, every thought that we have, is building and shaping what tomorrow is going to look like.

There is a great Scripture in the book of Haggai, and basically, it is God asking a question. When you walk out of your storm, you need to know what your harvest is going to look like. If you are in the middle of your storm, begin to sow seeds of what you want life to look like outside of the storm.

Every word is a seed. Every thought is a seed. And every action is a seed that builds our tomorrow. In the book of Haggai, God asks the question, "Is there seed in the barn (Haggai 2:9)?"

Is their seed in *your* barn? That question is really pretty simple. You plant seed that grows a harvest. But if your seed is in the barn, you are never going to get a harvest. And God is saying, "Why haven't you invested in your future?"

You have this whole barn full of seed, and God looks at you and says, "You are loaded with potential. Greater is He that is in you than he that is in the world (1 John 4:4). I know what I put within you. I know who you are. I know what you are like. My Spirit is in you. Why have you not begun to walk by faith, talk by faith, act by faith, or live by faith? Why is there still seed in the barn? You are not of the world, though you are in it. Come on out of it, and live like a person of faith."

Avoid Distractions

Finally, to rebuild after a storm, you have got to avoid distractions. All the time that Nehemiah was building the wall, there were distractions from the inside so that Nehemiah had to repeat the vision. Every so often, he would go back and say, "Guys, let me remind you why we're doing what we're doing. Let me remind you why we're here." There was this vision-drift on the inside, and there were outside forces, as well that were coming against them.

In fact, if you read the book of Nehemiah, you find out that he told the people, "Get up on the wall. Put a tool in one hand and a sword in the other. Keep building and keep fighting, but don't ever come down off the wall." Do not get distracted from what God is doing. Do not get distracted from building your life.

Jesus said, "No man putting his hand to the plough and looking back is fit for the Kingdom of God (Luke 9:62)." That simply means you cannot look forward and backward at the same time. Choose the direction that you are going. I love the statement, "Quit rehearsing what *has* happened, and start rehearsing what *can* happen." Discouragement is a distraction.

D. L. Moody made this statement: "You never judge a man's greatness by talent, wealth, or education. You judge a man's greatness by what it takes to discourage him." Discouragement, for the most part, is a choice. Now, before you get mad at me, let me try to explain. If you are discouraged, no one is holding a gun to your head and making you stay discouraged. You are as happy as you want to be.

Let me give an example. If I were to tell you, "If you'll get happy, I'll give you a million dollars at the end of the day," you would be the happiest person on earth. You just do not have enough motivation yet. But hasn't God promised so much more than that? Do not get distracted.

Satan will use people to distract you. He kept sending Sanballat to reason with Nehemiah and say, "Come down off the wall. Let's talk about this. Is this really what you need to be doing?" But Nehemiah would never stop and reason with him. God never told us to reason with the enemy. He said to resist him, not to play mind games with him, talk to him, or try to figure him out.

So, every time the devil shows up in your life in a negative way, a destructive way, or discouraging way, God said to resist him. Just quit thinking that direction, and put your thoughts and your focus on God.

Every wall in the Old Testament had what they called a watchman. The responsibility of the watchman, naturally, was to watch. He would stand up on the wall and look out over the horizon. If he saw anything that looked out of the ordinary, he would alert the city. If he saw a dust cloud, maybe he would think it was a dust of an approaching army, and he would warn everybody by blowing the trumpet.

You need to have a watchman on the wall, and that watchman is God's Spirit on the inside of you. There are things that God will alert you to and make you aware of by the Spirit. Remember that invisible side of life that I talked about? -getting plugged into that supernatural side of God, living both in the natural and the supernatural at the same time. That watchman on the wall is God speaking to you through the person of the Holy Spirit, directing your life and ordering your steps.

I will give you one last Scripture, and this is a great rebuilding Scripture. It is not enough just to know it, but we have to come to the place where, when we hear the Scripture, we don't just dismiss it, but we stop and think about it, saying either, "This is really true, and it is really what God is saying," or "I need to just tear that page out of my Bible." Here it is:

Romans 8:28

And we know all things work together for the good of those that love him and that are called according to his purpose.

Whatever the enemy has used to destroy you, God is going to use that to promote you. In fact, the plans of the enemy against your life are going to backfire. The word *backfire* means "to have the opposite effect of what it was intended to have." Whatever the enemy has planned for your life is going to have the opposite effect of what it was intended to have.

God is going to use those plans, those schemes, those events of the enemy, and He is going to turn them into your promotion and blessing. That is what He does. He is an expert at taking the brokenness of our life and putting it back together, reassembling it not like it was, but *better* than it ever was before.

Review

Nehemiah had a vision, examined the situation in Jerusalem, prayed, made a plan, got to work, and avoided distractions along the way. We can do the same.

I pray that you will come out of your storm stronger than you were before. My heart breaks for you if you have experienced loss along the way, and I know there might be people or things which cannot be recovered. However, God can put other pieces back together and give you a bright future. He can rebuild your life after a storm.

Take Action

1. If you have just gotten through a storm, write out a
   plan for rebuilding.

_____

_____

_____

_____

_____

2. Write out the things about the storm that you can
   thank God for. What did you learn? How have you
   been strengthened?

_____

_____

_____

_____

_____

CONCLUSION

We all face storms in life. Some are more painful than others, and some people seem to get a double dose of tragedy. Whatever difficulties you will experience, are experiencing, or have just experienced, my goal has been to give you some tools to help you come out victorious.

In Chapter One, we defined a STORM and gave some characteristics of storms. They are often sudden, but they are also temporary. Sometimes we did not do anything to bring them on, and sometimes we cause our own storms. But, in any case, God has given some anchors to help hold us steady when a storm is raging. Cling to your anchors of family and faith.

In Chapter Two, we talked about how to build your life on the solid foundation of God's Word. It is a daily practice, but if you do it, when the rain, floods, and winds come, you will be ready.

In Chapter Three, we focused on how to have a strong marriage. If you are married, the relationship with your spouse is of primary importance aside from your relationship with God. If your marriage is struggling, it will affect your whole life. So, work to put on rose-colored glasses, empty the drama box, communicate well, and show affection. If your marriage is strong, it can be an anchor to get you through storms.

In Chapter Four, I talked about how to master your money. Financial storms can also wreck your life and cause a lot of stress. Put God first in your finances, and watch what He can do. Pray for His help if you are in debt, and let him walk you out.

Chapter Five was all about worry. For some of you, worry seems to be a way of life, but worrying is telling God that you do not trust Him. Remember that God is on your side, He will never leave you, and He can work miracles in your life. There is simply no need to worry, and in that chapter, I gave some practical steps for overcoming it.

In Chapter Six, we took a look at how Jesus handled a major storm as He was heading to the cross. Depression is a common experience, and many prominent leaders in the Bible had times of depression. The question is what to do when you find yourself there. This chapter was not about clinical depression, but rather the depression that most people face when storms get especially tough. I listed some common causes of depression so you can get to the root of it.

Finally, Chapter Seven was about rebuilding after a storm. We took a close look at the life of Nehemiah and specifically saw how he approached rebuilding the city of Jerusalem. You can use that to build an action plan for rebuilding your life. Have a vision for the future, pray often, and avoid distractions as you work out your plan.

My prayer is that God has used this book to give you strength, focus, and ideas for getting through your most difficult moments. Do not give up. God is for you and is ready to help you.

If you need prayer, please reach out, and we would be happy to pray with you.

Cornerstone Church
9900 SE 15th
Midwest City, OK 73130
Phone: 405-737-5599
https://www.cornerstone.tv/
https://www.ronmckey.com/

REFERENCES

[1]Schuller, Robert. Tough Times Never Last, But Tough People Do. Thomas Nelson, 1983.

[2]McKay, Matthew and Patrick Fanning. *Successful Problem Solving: A* Workbook to Overcome the Four Core Beliefs That Keep You *Stuck.*New Harbinger Publications, 2002.

[3]Driscoll, Mark. Real Marriage: The Truth About Sex, Friendship, and Life *Together.* Thomas Nelson Publishing, 2012.

[4]Thomas, Gary. *Sacred Marriage.* Zondervan, 2000.

[5]Gusovski, Dina. "Americans Consume Vast Majority of the World's Opioids". CNBC.com
https://www.cnbc.com/2016/04/27/americans-consume-almost-all-of-the-global-opioid-supply.html

[6]Warren, Rick. Meet the Press Interview. November 29, 2009.
http://www.nbcnews.com/id/34079938/ns/meet_the_press/t/meet-press-transcript-nov/#.XmZ2lJNKhQI

[7]Borkovec, Thomas; Hazlett-Stevens, Holly; Diaz, M.L. "The Role of Positive Beliefs about Worry in Generalized Anxiety Disorder and its Treatment", Clinical Psychology & Psychotherapy. 1999.

The Holy Bible. King James Version, English Standard Version, New Living Translation, The Message Bible.

ABOUT THE AUTHOR

B eing pastors is more than a career choice for Ron and Carol McKey; it is a calling burning deep inside. It drives them to stay creative and relevant in communicating the life-changing message of Jesus Christ in an ever-changing culture that needs to see, hear and feel the love of God.

With over 35 years of experience pastoring children, youth, and adults, they have remained true to their purpose of reaching the entire family. Pastor Ron McKey communicates in a way that speaks to today's culture, focusing on how to apply Christ's teachings to our lives, so we can experience God's incredible purpose each and every day.

Carol, a graduate of Life Christian University, works closely with her husband to create and administrate the various ministries and events of Cornerstone Church. Together, they are committed to pastoring a community.

Made in the USA
Columbia, SC
20 March 2021